READER'S DIGEST
VISITORS' GUIDE
TO THE

GREAT

BARRIER

REEF

Some of the material in this book first appeared in
Reader's Digest Book of the Great Barrier Reef,
first published in 1984.

Devised, edited and designed by Mead & Beckett Publishing
Scientific consultant   Major photographer
Frank Talbot   Roger Steene

READER'S DIGEST
VISITORS' GUIDE TO THE
GREAT BARRIER REEF
was devised and edited by
Reader's Digest Services Pty Ltd

First edition
Published by Reader's Digest Services Pty Limited
(Inc. in NSW)
26-32 Waterloo Street, Surry Hills, NSW 2010
© 1988 Reader's Digest Services Pty Limited
© 1988 Reader's Digest Association Far East Limited
Philippines copyright 1988 Reader's Digest
Association Far East Limited
© 1988 Reader's Digest Association, Inc.
® Reader's Digest is a registered trade mark of
The Reader's Digest Association, Inc. of
Pleasantville, New York, USA

National Library of Australia
cataloguing-in-publication data

Visitors' guide to the Great Barrier Reef.
1st ed.
Includes index.
ISBN 0 86438 073 9.
1. Great Barrier Reef (Qld.) – Description
and travel – Guide-books. I. Reader's
Digest Services.
919.43'0463

Sea horse, *Hippocampus*

READER'S DIGEST VISITORS' GUIDE TO THE

GREAT BARRIER REEF

Reader's Digest, Sydney

Contributors

P. N. Alderslade, BSc
Curator of Coelenterates, Northern Territory
Museum of Arts and Sciences, Darwin.
Corals

Gordon R. V. Anderson, BSc, MSc
Principal Project Officer, Australian National Parks
and Wildlife Service, Canberra.
Conserving for the future

J. T. Baker, OBE, MSc, PhD, FRACI
Director, Sir George Fisher Centre for Tropical
Marine Studies, James Cook University of North
Queensland, Townsville.
Conserving for the future

A.A. Benson, PhD
Professor of Biology, Scripps Institution of
Oceanography, University of California, San Diego.
Symbiosis

R. Alastair Birtles, MA
Tutor in Marine Biology and Zoology, James Cook
University of North Queensland, Townsville.
Echinoderms

Harold G. Cogger, MSc, PhD
Deputy Director, Australian Museum, Sydney.
Marine reptiles

Alistair J. Gilmour, BSc, PhD, FTS
Executive Officer, Great Barrier Reef Marine Park
Authority, Townsville.
Conserving for the future

Barry Goldman, BSc, PhD
Director, Lizard Island Research Station, Great
Barrier Reef.
Fishes
Conserving for the future

Edward R. Lovell, MSc
Experimental Officer, Australian Institute of Marine
Science, Townsville.
Corals

H. D. Marsh, BSc, PhD
Research Fellow in Zoology, James Cook University
of North Queensland, Townsville.
Marine mammals

P. Saenger, BSc, PhD, FLS
Research Fellow, Department of Zoology,
University of New England, Armidale.
Diving and snorkelling

Frank H. Talbot, MSc, PhD, FRZS, FLS
Executive Director, California Academy of
Sciences, San Francisco.
24 hours on a coral reef
Fishes
Conserving for the future

Carden C. Wallace, PhD
Research Fellow, Department of Marine Biology,
James Cook University of North Queensland,
Townsville
Corals

C. R. Wilkinson, BSc, PhD
Senior Research Scientist, Australian Institute of
Marine Science, Townsville.
Sponges

We extend grateful thanks to the Australian Institute
of Marine Science for granting permission to use
their material.

We also gratefully acknowledge the assistance of the
Australian Museum, and the following people: Janice
Aldenhoven, Dustin Chivers, Phil Coleman, Paul
Dixon, Dr William Eschmeyer, Linda Gibson,
William Gladstone, Dr Andrew C. Heron, Dr Doug
Hoese, Dr James Lowry, Dr John McCosker,
Paulette McWilliam, Susan Middleton, Randolph
Olson, Dr John Paxton, Dr Stuart Poss, Dr Frank
Rowe, Dr Peter Sale, Dr Roger Springthorpe and
Hugh Sweatman.

Photographers

(Abbreviations: a = above, b = below, c = centre,
l = left, r = right, t = top.)

P. Alderslade: 64 br, 65 bl and r. **Gary Bell/P & O
Resorts:** 150 l. **D. Bellwood:** 89 r. **A. A. Benson:**
101 t, r and bl. **G. Biddle:** 99. **M. Bryden:** 137 bl.
Neville Coleman: 89 tl. **David Colfelt:** 134.
Ben Cropp: 139. **D'Arcy Masius Benton &
Bowles P/L (Melb.):** 149 tr, 150 br, 158, 159 r,
160 l, 161. **Daydream Island Marketing:** 151 l,
152 t, 153 b. **Z. Dineson:** 84 br. **T. Done:** 92 l
and br. **Far North Queensland Promotion
Bureau:** 157 r. **D. Fisk:** 88 tr. **Fojo/courtesy of
Jackson Studios:** 156 l. **Fojo/Craig Lamotte:** 147,
151 br, 154 l, 156 c and r, 157 l. **Barry Goldman:**
14 r. **GBR Marine Park Authority:** 136 l.
Hamilton Island Enterprises P/L: 153 tr, 154 r.
P. Harrison: 78 tr and br, 80 bl, 81 tl, 82 l and br.
Hayles Holdings P/L: 159 l, 160 tr, 162 b. **George
Heinsohn:** 136 r. **A. Heywood:** 80 t. **David
Hopley:** 148. **Jim Hudnall:** 135. **Intrasun
Australia P/L:** 149 tl. **Lady Musgrave Barrier
Reef Cruises:** 149 cl, cr and b. **E. Lovell:** 64 bl, 69
bl, 70 l, 72 la, l, ra and r, 73 tl, tr, cr, bl and bc, 74 ct, c,
cr and br, 76 la and br, 83 bl and br, 84 tr, 85 bl, 86 br
and tr, 87, 88 l, 89 bl, 90 r, 91 bl, 92 tr, 93 b, 94 b, 95 r,
96 l and r, 97 tl, cl, bl and r. **C. MacDonald:** 137 r.
Leo Meier/Weldon Trannies: 155 b. **Mitchell
Library:** 141. **National Geographic:** 100.
J. Oliver: 78 la and lb. **Orpheus Island Marketing:**
162 t, 163. **D. Parer:** 138 t. **Queensland Tourist
and Travel Corporation:** 150 tr, 151 tr, 152 b,
153 tl. **David B. Simmonds/courtesy Hayman
Resorts:** 155 t. **Roger Steene:** Endpapers, 1, 3, 5, 6,
7, 16 l and r, 17 l and br, 18 l and r, 19 a, l and r, 20 a, l
and r, 21 l and r, 23 b, 24 l and lb, 25 r, 26 l and r, 27
al, l, ar and r, 28 al, l and r, 29, 30, 31 a and b, 32, 33 bl
and r, 34 b, 36 bl and r, 37 la, l and r, 39, 40 l and r, 41
tl, tr and br, 42 tr and br, 43 l, 45 a and b, 46 l, cb and
br, 47, 48 tl and br, 49 la, l and r, 50, 52 la, lb, ra and
rb, 53 a and b, 54 br, 55 la, lb, ra and rb, 56 bl and r,
57, 59, 60, 61, 62 b, 63 l, r and b, 64 l and ar, 65 l, 66 l,
c, ar and br, 67 a and b, 68 l, a and b, 69 al, cb and r,
70 tr and br, 71 a and b, 73 al, cl, bl, c and br, 74 l, cb
and tr, 75 l, ar and r, 76 bl and ar, 77 l, al, r and ab, 79
tl, tr, c and b, 80 br, 81 bl and br, 82 tr, 84 l, 85 tl and
r, 88 c, 90 l, 91 r, 93 t, 94 t, 95 l and al, 98, 102, 103,
104 l and r, 105 l, la and r, 106, 107 tl, tr and br, 108 l,
t and r, 109 a and b, 110, 111 l, 112 l, t, bl and br, 113
t, c and br, 114 l, al, r and ar, 115 l, al, r and ar, 116 bl
and tr, 117 tl, ac and r, 118, 119 tl and bl, 120 l, t and
r, 122 l and r, 123 t, bl and br, 124 tl, cl, r and br, 125 a
and b, 126 a and b, 127 al, l and r, 128 a and b, 129 tl,
l, tr and r, 132, 133 r, 137 tl, 138 b, 140, 142, 143 l and
r, 145. **Frank Talbot:** 14 t and bl, 15 a and b, 58, 62 t,
107 bl. **Valerie Taylor:** 121 t. **B. Willis:** 83 t. **Eric
Wolanski:** 160 br. **Bill Wood:** 12, 13, 17 tr, 22, 23 t,
24 r, 25 l, 33 tl, 34 t, 35, 36 tl and br, 38, 41 bl, 42 l, 43
r, 44 tl, c, b and r, 46 tr and c, 48 tr, 51 a and b, 54 tr
and l, 56 tl, 73 ca, 91 tl, 106, 111 r, 113 bl, 116 tl and
br, 117 bl, 119 r, 121 b, 130, 131 l and r, 133 l.

Diagrams

Leonie Bremer-Kamp: 61 r, 62 l.

Maps

Mercury-Walch: 8-11.

Page one: The male blue-headed wrasse, Thalassoma
amblycephalus, *is found throughout the reef waters. The
female has a white belly and a dark blue back, covered
with thin black bands.*

Page three: The fabled sea horse, Hippocampus, *is one of
the strangest and most appealing of the reef's creatures. The
female lays her clutch of eggs in a special pouch on the
male's abdomen and leaves him with the responsibility.*

Page five: This prolific genus of stony coral, Acropora,
*with its herd of blue damselfish, is the dominant coral on
most reefs. The growth form varies from delicate branches
to plate-like formations.*

Contents

Shrimp, *Rhynchocinetes*

An introduction to the Great Barrier Reef

There are a few places in the world which fulfil the meaning of the word 'enchantment'. They not only delight the senses, but they cast a spell which can even affect the behaviour of human beings. Most of us are monsters to whom self-interest is the main motif of life. Only beauty and power of a remarkable order can charm us into forgetting our interests and doing battle on its behalf. The Great Barrier Reef is one place which has that power.

The reef survives today, without the industrial threat of oil rigs and mineral exploitation and consequent killing pollution, because of this power. The years in which people first took on the battle to have the reef protected from unsympathetic exploitation and declared a Marine National Park are long ago now, and some of those who worked on its side are old or dead. But the remarkable factor in its rescue was the near-unanimity of Queenslanders, and indeed most other Australians, that it should not be spoiled. Once the issues were made clear, many who had never seen it or scarcely knew more of it than reports and photographs joined in the public outcry on its behalf. It would not now be politically possible to reverse the decision that the reef will be protected from the grosser forms of exploitation as a Marine Park – though there are many other threats to its continuing existence, it will not be thrown to the modern dragons quite so carelessly. It has cast a spell, and the people who know it and whom it has enchanted will continue to work on its behalf.

The Great Barrier Reef is perhaps the only such place which lies mainly under water and is therefore not accessible except at certain times and seasons. This is part of its mystery. Also, it is alive – the summits of those underwater mountains teem with life of an unbelievable variety of colour, pattern, form, function and interaction. It is this *livingness* that makes the reef so much more than a mere 'place'. Every isolated cay and shore, the barrier ramparts and the tidal pools, move and sway and dart with living creatures. The beauty of the earth – mountains, forests, cultivated landscapes, icefields, deserts – is not like this; such places are static, accessible, inhabited by warm-blooded creatures like ourselves for the most part and therefore familiar sharers in our breathable atmosphere. But the underwater world is still alien. Its inhabitants live on different terms from ours, and we have only recently been able to explore it in comparative safety. The lives of its inhabitants are unsharable – we have nothing in common with them except life itself. This gives to the reef a strangeness which adds a special dimension to its beauty.

My own knowledge and experience of the Great Barrier Reef is comparatively small – a holiday on Heron Island, and a much earlier few weeks in the immediate postwar years on Lady Elliot Island, the reef's southernmost coral cay, then inhabited only by a little colony of lighthouse keepers. It is Lady Elliot Island which has left the deepest memory with me, though even then it had been devastated by the visits of guano-seeking ships and by a herd of goats kept as a meat supply for the lighthouse staff. Yet its fringing reef had survived all this and the sea which surrounded the island was brilliantly clean and dazzling-clear. 'When I remember it', I wrote more than thirty years later, in *Australia's Natural Heritage*, 'my inner eye is flooded with those marvellous blues and greens of unpolluted water; and the coral pools at low tide held millions of little fishes, anemones, stars, urchins, holothurians, shellfish, crabs, sponges and coral species, all apparently trying to outdo each other in elegance and beauty of pattern, form and colour'.

On calm days we could row out over the fringing reef to look down the crags of coral into valleys and down walls where dim, many-coloured seaweeds and branching growths of coral harboured thousands of other organisms, and shoals of larger fishes, squid, octopus, manta rays and sharks swam. Farther out, whales still blew great fountains on the horizon, dolphins somersaulted and undulated in cheerful processions, and everywhere sea birds hunted the skies – from the big white-breasted sea eagles to the little terns.

All these teeming and changing lifescapes – to coin a term – visible under and over the glowing blues of a tropical sea, seemed to demand interpretation in terms more accessible than the Latin nomenclature most of them were saddled with. But the only poet who has specifically tried to write in and of the reef and its non-human inhabitants – Mark O'Connor, who has lived on it, dived on it, and been instructed in terminology by scientists working on its research stations – has almost despaired of the limitations of an English language evolved in cold northern latitudes and of a Latin system of nomenclature to express the life of the reef. It is hard to find a way of conveying, say, the character and beauty of a spectacular creature whose name is *Euborlasia quinquestriata*, which has been seen by few people, and which has no common name except 'ribbon worm' – and there are many different species of ribbon worms. Roses and nightingales, even waratahs and magpies, are easier poet-fodder. It may be a long while before the reef has a literature of its own.

Since my own first visit to the southernmost part of the reef, there has been much change. Where in 1949 few people visited it and tourist resorts were few and far between, the accessibility of much of the area by petrol-driven launches, tourist ships and helicopters has brought it into the ambit of world tourism. Diving and spearfishing equipment, big-game fishing and the rest of the modern introductions whose impacts on the reef and its waters are still unknown, have thrown it at our mercy, and its days of peace are not likely to return. While zoning plans and educative projects will help, the future of the reef lies with *people*. A rising population, a rising tourist industry, onshore pollution and many other factors threaten it. How to educate for reverence and respect? Our record is not good; but at least we have made a start. The Great Barrier Reef is perhaps the most important, certainly one of the most beautiful and significant, gifts Australia has given the world by nominating it as a World Heritage possession.

JUDITH WRIGHT

Aboriginal cave painting

△ *Aborigines have lived in Australia for more than 40 000 years. From their earliest occupation of the continent they had a knowledge of the sea and its inhabitants, which they recorded in cave paintings.*

◁ *This colourful shrimp is a member of a diverse family found throughout the Indo-Pacific region. Many forms live within the corals and are active mainly at night.*

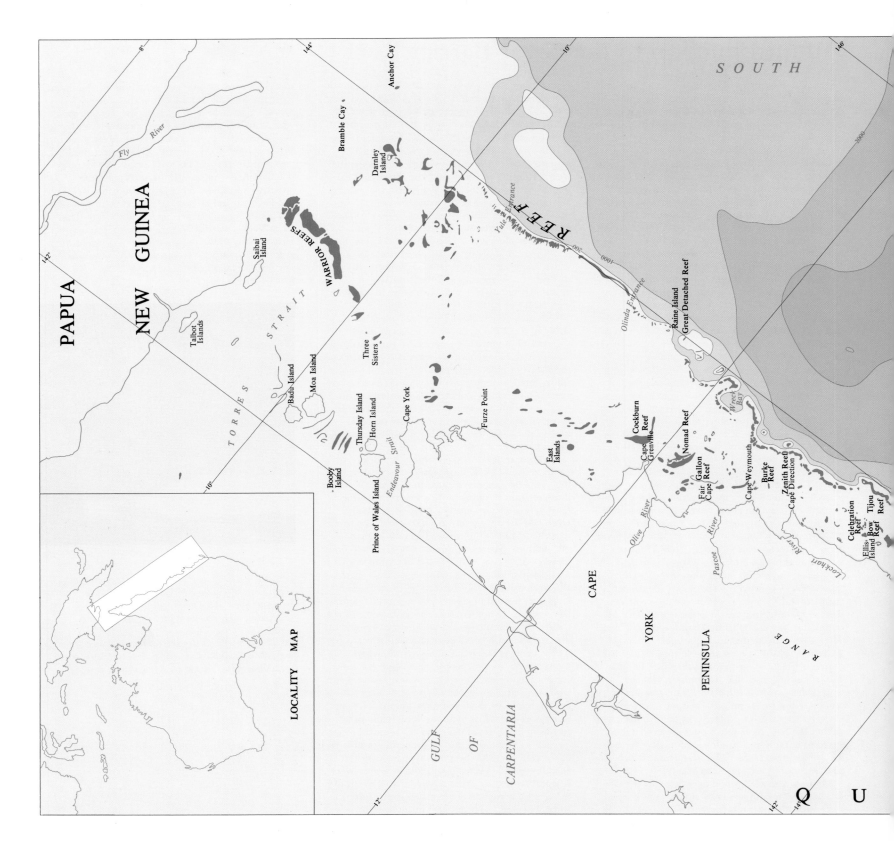

SOUTH

PAPUA

NEW GUINEA

Fly River

Anchor Cay

Bramble Cay

Darnley Island

Saibai Island

WARRIOR REEFS

REEF

Yule Entrance

Olinda Entrance

Raine Island
Great Detached Reef

Talbot Islands

T O R R E S   S T R A I T

Badu Island

Moa Island

Three Sisters

Thursday Island

Horn Island

Cape York

Furze Point

East Islands

Cockburn Reef

Cape Grenville

Nomad Reef

Wreck Bay

Booby Island

Prince of Wales Island

Endeavour Strait

Fair Cape

Gallon Reef

Cape Weymouth

Burke Reef

Zenith Reef

Cape Direction

Olive River

Pascoe River

Celebration Reef

Tijou Reef

Ellis Island

Bow Reef

Lockhart River

CAPE

YORK

PENINSULA

R A N G E

GULF

OF

CARPENTARIA

LOCALITY   MAP

Q

U

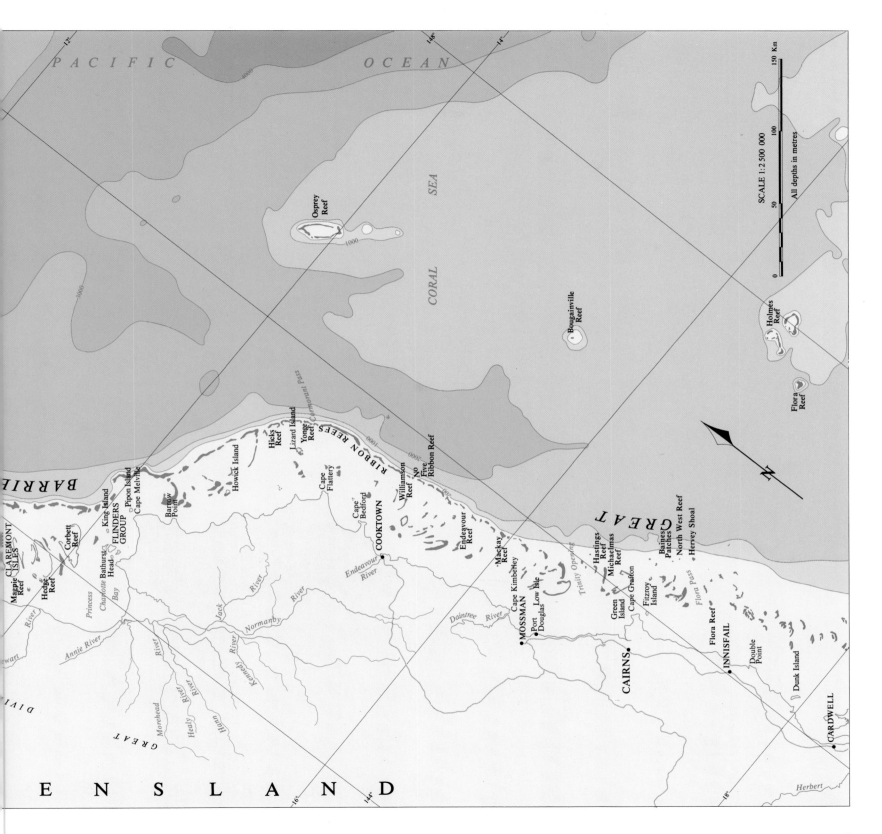

PACIFIC   OCEAN

CORAL   SEA

Osprey
Reef

Bougainville
Reef

Holmes
Reef

Flora
Reef

SCALE 1:2 500 000

All depths in metres

N

Cormorant Pass

RIBBON REEFS

Lizard Island
Yonge Reef
Hicks
Reef
Howick Island

Cape
Flattery

Williamson
Reef
No
Five
Ribbon Reef

BARRIER

King Island
Pipon Island
Cape Melville
FLINDERS
GROUP

Barrow
Point

Cape
Bedford

Endeavour
Reef

GREAT

Baines
Patches
North West Reef
Hervey Shoal

Corbett
Reef
Bathurst
Head
CLAREMONT ISLES

Magpie
Reef
Hedge
Reef

Charlotte
Bay

Princess

Mackay
Reef

Cape Kimberley
Low Isle
Port
Douglas

Trinity Opening

Hastings
Reef
Michaelmas
Reef

Green
Island
Cape Grafton

Fitzroy
Island

Flora Pass

COOKTOWN

Endeavour River

MOSSMAN

Daintree   River

CAIRNS

Flora Reef

INNISFAIL

Double
Point

Dunk Island

River

River

Jack

Normanby

River

Annie River

Stewart

Kennedy
River

Hedly River

Hann
River

Morehead
River

GREAT

DIVI

E   N   S   L   A   N   D

Herbert

CARDWELL

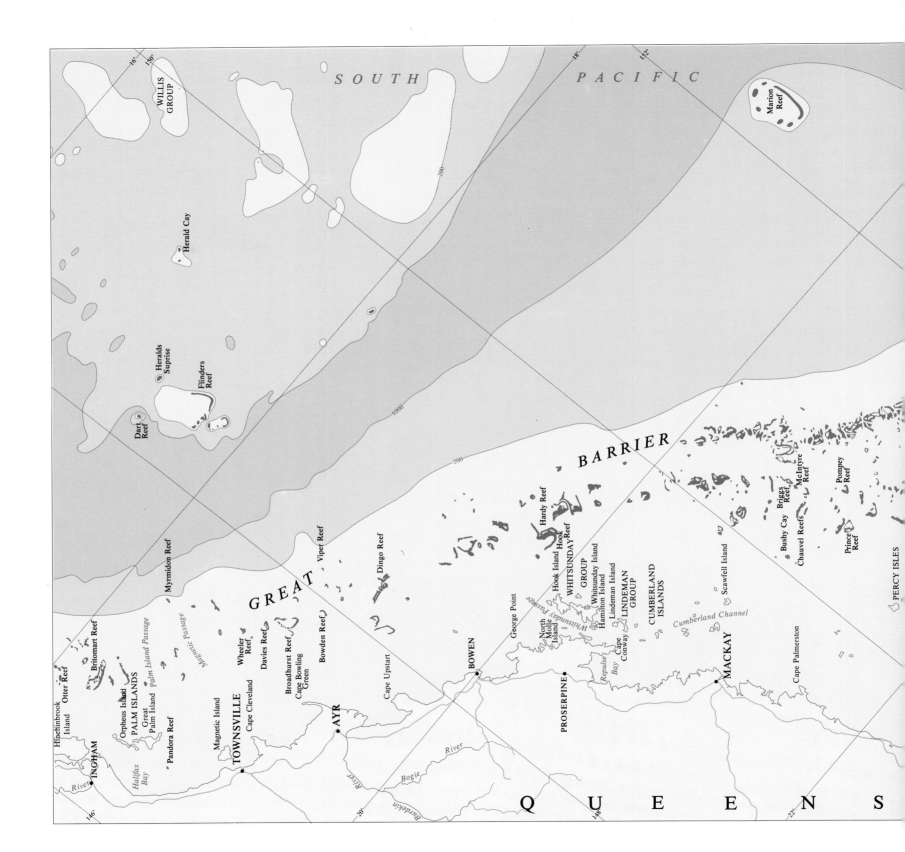

SOUTH PACIFIC

WILLIS GROUP

Marion Reef

Herald Cay

Heralds Suprise

Flinders Reef

Dart Reef

BARRIER

Myrmidon Reef

Hardy Reef

Briggs Reef

McIntyre Reef

Pompey Reef

GREAT

Viper Reef

Dingo Reef

Hook Island Hook
WHITSUNDAY Reef
Hook Island
WHITSUNDAY GROUP
Whitsunday Island
Lindeman Island
LINDEMAN GROUP
CUMBERLAND ISLANDS

Bushy Cay

Chauvel Reefs

Prince Reef

PERCY ISLES

Britomart Reef

Otter Reef

Orpheus Island
PALM ISLANDS
Great Palm Island
Palm Island Passage

Magnetic Passage

Wheeler Reef

Davies Reef

Broadhurst Reef
Cape Bowling Green

Bowden Reef

Cape Upstart

George Point

North Molle Island

Whitsunday Passage

Repulse Bay
Cape Conway
Hamilton Island
Cape Palmerston

Scawfell Island

Cumberland Channel

Hinchinbrook Island

Pandora Reef

Magnetic Island
TOWNSVILLE
Cape Cleveland

BOWEN

PROSERPINE

MACKAY

INGHAM

AYR

Halifax Bay

River

Bogie River

Burdekin River

QUEENS

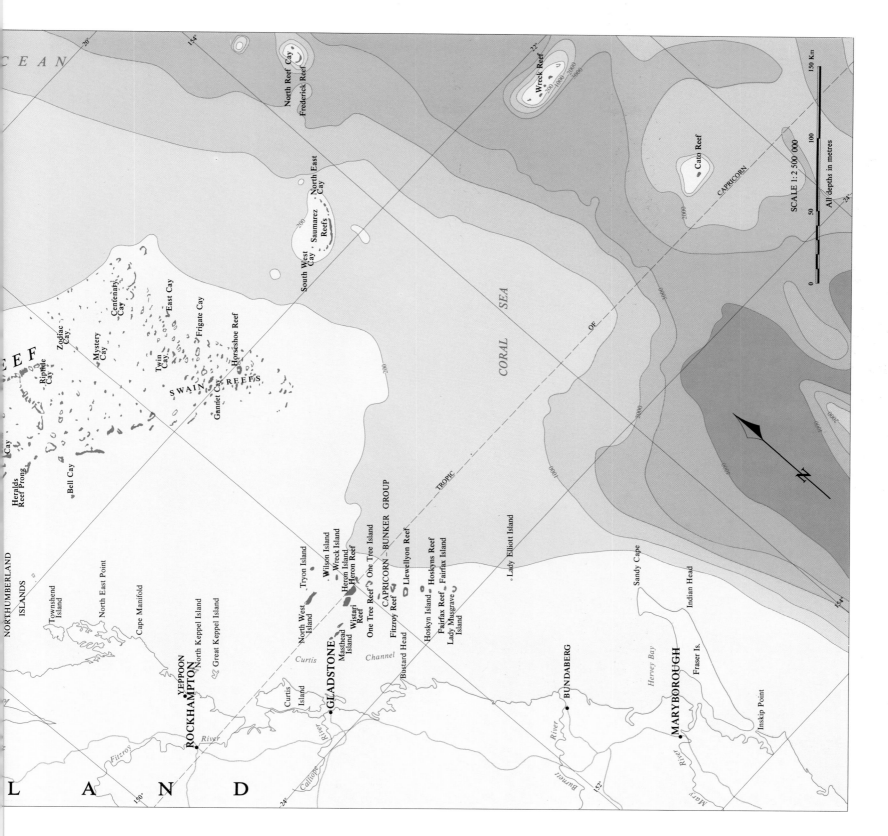

MAP OF THE GREAT BARRIER REEF   11

Silver gull, *Larus novaehollandiae*

Part one: 24 hours on a coral reef

The underwater world of the Great Barrier Reef follows a unique day and night pattern, influenced by the coming and going of the high tropical sun and the twice-daily rise and fall of the tides. Reef organisms of breathtaking colour and variety have evolved a delicate balance of hunters and prey, camouflage and brilliant display, competing with each other for space and feeding time, yet accommodating themselves to the reef's great rhythms. A morning dive, and then another at dusk, enable us to watch an amazing cycle of change and re-formation.

The morning dive

It is dawn over the Great Barrier Reef. We carry our gear over smooth, cool sand and load the boat just as the sun breaks through a layer of those little cotton-wool clouds, now grey below and tinged with gold above, that seem to be always on the horizon and seldom above you in the tropical sky. The tide is very low and the surface so still that it reflects the green hill on the island and the clouds sailing high above it.

Everywhere the reefs are above the surface, and the reef crest makes a long line at the outer edge of the lagoon with only a few gaps where the water gently sucks in and out. The exposed reefs will shelter us from even a hint of the Coral Sea swell. Out on the reef flat an egret is already hunting on his low-tide territory, white plumes tinged yellow by the sun and its reflection in the still pools.

▷ *Hungry after a night's sleep, a grey reef egret waits for the falling tide to expose its feeding places on the reef flat. This species – either slate grey or pure white – searches for food over the whole area exposed at low tide, each in its own territory, often using its wings to shade the pool so that its sharp eyes can see the fishes and shellfish below without reflections. Though it roosts in groups, each bird occupies and vigorously defends its own territory on the reef at low tide. It often stands motionless by the water with its head sunk onto its shoulders.*

◁ *A scavenging silver gull, the opportunist of the reef's islands and cays, pauses in the dawn light. During the breeding season the gulls steal eggs or chicks from careless birds of other species. The hatching period of young turtles is also a feast time, for gulls wait in noisy groups and take the youngsters as they make their dash for the sea. But at low tide they also hunt the sands and the exposed reefs for scraps, perhaps of some predator/prey battle of a few hours before, or for small dead animals from the plankton that have washed ashore.*

'Early dawn on the reef. The air is cool and clean with the city far away. The scene is so untouched and splendid that it could be pre-man.'

Eastern reef egret, *Ardea sacra*

◁ More than a few hours of exposure will kill the
corals. They produce heavy mucus that helps to prevent
dehydration and that can be easily seen as a surface slick
floating away with the rising tide. A giant clam lies
completely exposed but comes to no harm. This has
happened many times before and the slow-growing clam
has probably been here for a hundred years or more.

Giant clam, *Tridacna gigas*

△ At extreme low tide on the reef on a lovely morning
the water is crystal clear and the exposed coral shows
wonderful sculptured shapes and colour. A day like this is
ideal for diving or just wading through the shallows
watching the life in and about the corals.

◁ Still pools at the reef crest. Even in this protected reef
the water at the outer edge of the reef flat is usually
turbulent. A combination of very low tide and lack of
wind results in a glassy surface, with exposed shrub,
staghorn and plate or tabular corals. As the tide rises this
area will be grazed by surgeon and parrotfish, for there is
much algal turf at the bases of and between these corals.
At present these grazers are over the reef crest, waiting
and feeding in deeper water.

Shrub, staghorn and plate coral, *Acropora*

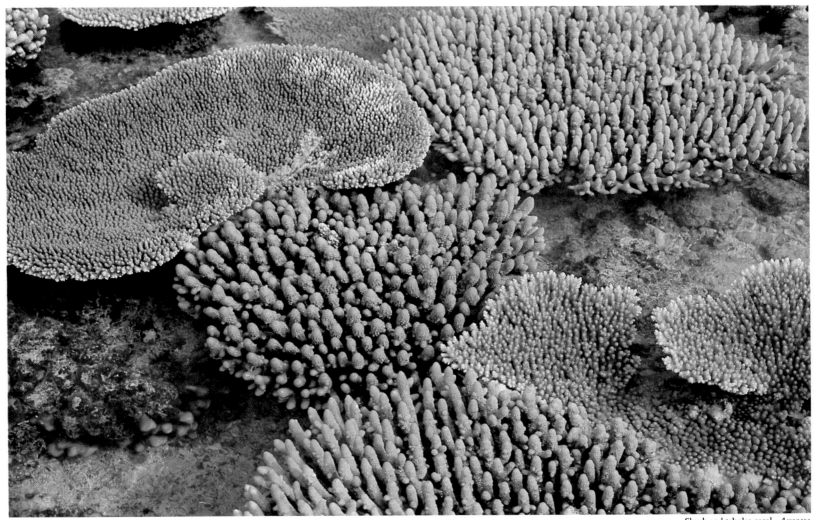

Shrub and tabular coral, *Acropora*

Splendour at low tide

'Exposed reefs at extreme low tides are rare and offer danger to the coral that will be harmed by long exposure. At certain times of the year, large areas of reef may be exposed to atmospheric conditions for some hours each day.'

Shrub and tabular coral, *Acropora*

△ *These corals, above and left, seen so clearly in the low tide show a variety of growth patterns. Some are tabular, plate-like structures while others show typical branching shrub forms. The Acroporidae encompasses more species than any other family of corals. They have varied growth forms, porous skeletons and tiny polyps, rarely more than two millimetres in diameter. These corals grow well in shallow water.*

▷ *Large sponges are also more abundant on the reef base, apparently able to find a foothold where the light-loving corals start thinning. These tall tubes have small pores on the outer walls of the tube through which they draw water. This is filtered for food as it passes through the body, then enters the central tube and is exhaled through the open top. The process is aided by the currents that sweep along the reef and draw water out of the sponge tube.*

Tubular sponge

Sea whips, *Junceella*

△ *At the bottom of the reef sea whips dominate. Black coral, sea whips and sea fans of different types inhabit the deeper water of the reef. The scenery differs from the reef above and there is a new fauna of shrimps and small transparent gobies living on the sea whips.*

Even without wind the temperature is cool. Although we know that the water temperature over the outer reef edge changes little from night to day, a morning dive always seems cold at first. The small outboard motor pushes the boat across the shallow lagoon and through a gap in the reef crest to the open water beyond, where we look for a convenient place to explore on the rich slopes of the outer reef. The air is cool and clean and the city seems far away. As we stand with bare feet on crisp sand, it seems that no one else has ever been here, and the reef is utterly deserted.

Sea whip country

Clumsy in the boat in diving gear, we become weightless as we sink down the sloping face of the reef past a great jutting coral, to rest on soft sand twelve metres below. Here we are in sea whip country where the long whip-like horny corals spiral outwards from the coral rock above us. They have their own fauna: specially adapted, minute fishes – some of the smallest vertebrates in the world – cling to their stalks, along with shrimps. The little gobies are transparent and difficult to see, but if we put our hands round the base of a sea whip and gently move it, we will probably find a small goby skimming along in front of it.

Down below on the sandy slope a few feathery sea pens are visible, but the surface has mounds and small holes; it is a burrowing annexe of the reef, with many worms, crustaceans and molluscs living on the base. We now see a burrowing sea anemone

with delicate tentacles trailing in the slight current. At the slightest touch it will draw back into its fibrous tube and disappear.

The coral slope

The cold greyness of the early dawn is slowly lightening and the soft, warm colours of the corals start to show. We rise a little off the sea bed, adjusting our compensators to be able to hang motionless above the reef slope. Like the heron on the reef flat, the great mass of fishes that have rested overnight deep in the coral are hungry now and are leaving their 'beds' to start the day's foraging. Small sleepy fishes hang above the coral heads, wrasses and goatfish begin searching for food between the coral and the coral trout appear. Along the whole reef face there is movement. Looking up we can see the pale green-blue undersides of the small waves and their lazy splash where the reef breaks the surface.

'Along the whole reef face there is movement – clinging, spiralling and drifting.'

▷ *From below water the waves breaking on the reef crest create patterns of reflection and translucence, with colours of sky blue, turquoise and foam white, that constantly change and fascinate. Wave action during cyclones can be damaging to the reef. Large portions of branching coral colonies can be broken off, and sometimes whole blocks of coral are removed.*

Sea pen, *Pteroides*

△ *Below the reef is a steep sandy slope full of worms, crustaceans, molluscs, sea pens and anemones. Minute copepods shelter near rubble from the reef above, and schools of tiny, translucent possum shrimps, each about five millimetres long, can be found in hollows. Further down the slope wonderful feathery sea pen plumes, bravely held at right angles to the current, sift the water for small plankton.*

▷ *This sea anemone lives on the sandy mud below the reef. It has a tube into which it can withdraw with lightning speed if touched. Looking like a gentle flower, its long delicate tentacles waft with the current. But the stinging cells in the animal's tentacles are for serious food gathering and cause instant death to any small creature that sweeps into them.*

Sea anemone, *Cerianthid*

A tangle of corals

'Huge, rounded corals with eroded, undercut bases form holes and caverns that afford shelter for fishes. The seaward slopes of reefs are where the greatest and most virile coral growth occurs, but in deeper water, erosion is faster than growth.'

△ *Early morning on the reef base, above and right. The water here is too deep for a rich growth of sun-loving corals. They are replaced by a number of sea whips, sea fans and black corals with flexible skeletons that wave when the water is disturbed, unlike their stony shallow-water counterparts. Black corals are not black for, when alive, their flesh is actually yellow, orange, brown or grey. The 'black' skeleton, which is really very dark brown, is visible only after the animal's flesh is scrubbed off. Black coral is sought after for jewellery.*

Siphongorgia, sea whips and sea fans

Gorgonian, sea whips, sea fan and feather star

◁ *A tangle of horny corals is found with a large sea fan that has grown at right angles to the current flow along the reef, and strains microscopic food from the constantly washing water. A feather star clings here for its own feeding. Most sea fans, black corals and sea whips favour deeper levels where the water is cooler and the sunlight greatly reduced.*

Plate coral, *Acropora hyacinthus*; feather star, *Comatulids*

△ *Plate corals found in channels and protected areas, or in moderately deep water below the worst of the wave action, will sometimes grow to over two metres in diameter. But they can never live too deep; they need light strong enough for those algal food factories, the zooxanthellae, to produce enough food for vigorous coral growth. Here many species live permanently or shelter temporarily under a plate coral. Several feather stars are perched under this plate coral, but at night may be seen on top of it, arms extended, to net their fill of plankton.*

◁ *Nocturnal fishes return to shelter under their protective overhang after the night's feeding. The entrance of this cave is dominated by a rich growth of black coral.*

Black coral, *Antipathes*

Branching and plate coral, *Acropora*

Corals, *Porites*

'The great mass of fishes that have rested overnight deep in the coral are hungry in the morning and leave their beds to start the day's foraging.'

◁ *On the coral slope the early morning light is reflected through the small waves. A full cover of living coral is on the slope, and a mass of small daylight plankton feeders seek food after the fast of the night.*

Plate coral, *Acropora*

△ *A school of harlequin-coloured fishes fin gently above the coral at the base of the slope. These plate-like corals are some of the most beautiful on the reef. Related to the spectacular staghorns, they often occur together.*

◁ *It is still not fully understood what environmental subtleties create the varied patterns of the reef. Here the shrubby Acropores and their plate-shaped relatives have given way to species of solid boulder form. Some of these may grow over hundreds of years to colonies three to five metres in height.*

Anthiids

△ *At the base of the slope there may be small cliffs, overhangs and caverns. The erosive forces of the reef have overtaken reef growth, aided in some cases by wave action at earlier lower sea levels. Fishes of the night may shelter, sometimes in huge numbers, in these caverns.*

◁ *Where conditions of light or current are less suitable for stony corals, the surface is covered with other life – soft corals, encrusting algae, sponges and sea squirts. These small pink anthiids, relatives of the big rock cods, usually prefer deeper water.*

A solid, colourful mass

The corals on this outer slope are spectacular. Sweeping up to the reef crest is a great bank of shrub, staghorn and plate-like corals – many species of soft blues, pinks and greens forming a solid colourful mass. Total coral cover of the bottom is unusual, for normally the coral shrubs are separated by dead compacted coral rock, covered in either a fine algal turf or a hard, cement-like pink surface – also, surprisingly, encrusting algae. Here, this full coral cover is probably due to many factors, including currents, food and a wave action that is never great because of the shelter given by nearby reefs. The sloping bank of coral is punctuated by huge, rounded *Porites* corals with eroded, undercut bases that form holes and caverns large enough for us to enter. It has taken hundreds of years for the coral to grow to this size.

Colours of daylight

At full light, all the day species are about. Hundreds of fishes hang above the coral slope, a bewildering kaleidoscopic display of colour and form – large and small, elongated and chubby, with colours from hard black to translucent pink, yellow, orange, red, purple, blue and shimmering silver. There is nothing on land to compare with this variety:

Population explosion

'Daylight brings out an enormous variety of fish species – sometimes as many as 150 different kinds can be seen within the space of 100 square metres.'

White stinging hydroid, *Lytocarpus philippinus*

Puller fish, *Chromis atripectoralis*

△ *Growing on the lower slope is a hydroid with striking sprays of white fronds. This is one of the most beautiful of the soft hydroids, but it stings!*

▷ *A large school of young fishes on the reef edge are silhouetted against the morning light. Sometimes fishes settle from their planktonic phase in very large numbers.*

▷△ *Small damselfish or pullers sleep deep in the coral branches at night, but even while feeding during the day they stay close to their coral shelter.*

Damselfish

Sweetlip emperor, *Lethrinus chrysostomus*

△ Sweetlip emperors start to feed actively at dusk and are an angler's favourite. They grow up to 900 millimetres in length and their alternate name is 'tricky snapper'.

◁ Paddle-tail hussars school, keeping very close to the sea bed, and seem to pour over the surface following each hummock or dip. They live in shallow waters, feeding at dusk and in the early morning.

Paddle-tail hussar, *Lutjanus gibbus*

'There are more species of fishes on a coral reef than in any other place in the sea.'

Football trout, *Plectropomus melanoleucus*

Hawkfish, *Parachirrites forsteri*

Yellow-banded hussar, *Lutjanus amabilis*

△ *A hawkfish sits firmly on the coral. This little predator never hangs above the sea bed as most fishes do, but is always on the surface or tucked into a fork of coral.*

△△ *The colours of this close relative of the coral trout, the football trout, are similar to a football jersey. Its habits are like those of the coral trout, and it has sometimes been considered merely a colour variant. But it is not as common as the coral trout.*

schools of damsels like delicate moving clouds, wrasses, butterfly fish, parrotfish, hussars, sweetlips, small groupers and triggerfish. Where else does one find a hundred and fifty living species within a hundred square metres?

Feeding on the reef

Three large coral trout also hang over the coral slope, seemingly in harmony with the other fishes, but they are waiting for an unwary move by one of their prey – a fish too close, or too far from coral shelter. The potential prey go normally about their feeding, but with one eye on the big-mouthed trout. When a coral trout takes a fish, it happens in a flash – not a long rush, but a swift lunge and a suck – while the rest of the school continue feeding as though nothing has happened.

About fifty large yellow-banded hussars laze quietly around a huge undercut coral, resting. They are night feeders, but there is little doubt that if a tasty small fish came too close they would snap it up regardless of the time of day. Many night-hunting and dawn-and-dusk hunting species will find rest and protection in a school, quietly swimming to and fro near good shelter.

The outer slope is a rich area for plankton feeders. The ocean water, carrying its living load of minute plankton, washes through the reefs, restlessly pushed and pulled by tide and wind. A number of species of fusilier feed off the reef edge above the coral, sometimes in small groups, but often in large schools. And tiny damselfish pick the minute animals in the plankton. They leave their sheltering coral for food but never go far. There must always be the temptation to move further out from shelter upstream to get the drifting morsel before your neighbour. But go too far, and you will end in a trevally's maw.

'A large coral trout may stay around one area of coral for weeks, or even months, and then move off somewhere else, where the feeding is better.'

◁ *Yellow-banded hussars often school on the outer reefs during the day and hunt singly over the lagoon floor at night, protected by the darkness.*

▷ *A school of grazing parrotfish works, heads down, bumping at the coral and at each bump scraping the surface with their strong beaks. They keep the whole reef cropped, and seem to cover any dead rock or coral base each day. The drab-coloured individuals are in their female phase, and the brightly coloured fish are in the male phase. Parrotfish begin life as females and have at least one reproductive season before turning into males.*

▽ *The island coral trout is a wily predator, swimming out in the open with its prey, seemingly harmless and drifting slowly over the coral. But this one may well be about to attack. It has distinctive, bright blue markings on the head, cheeks and gill cover, with the rest of its body being reddish brown or grey. At least five species of coral trout are found on reefs in northern Australia.*

Parrotfish, *Scarus frenatus*

Island coral trout, *Plectropoma maculatum*

Hungry algal feeders

The grazers, chiefly schools of variously coloured parrotfish and sombre dark surgeons, are still being kept from the reef crest by the low tide and are scraping the algal-covered bases of the living corals and dead coral rock just below the gentle surge at the reef's edge. The parrotfish – a mixed school of different species and different colour phases – hang, with their tails up, bumping the surface as they take algae and dead coral with their hard beaks. The bristle-toothed surgeonfish eat more delicately, not leaving the bare scrape marks characteristic of the parrots. These fish grazers seem to cover every part of the surface daily – if we protect a piece of rock with wire mesh, its algae grow several centimetres long within a few days. Little of the algal turf along the reef's ten thousand kilometres is untouched by the hungry algal feeders.

As we get close to the reef an aggresive black damselfish guarding its territory rushes at us, a goliath twenty thousand times its weight. On top of a rock a blenny, with comical face and one swivelling eye, watches us as it hops about its small territory. While most fishes have a gas-filled swim bladder that keeps them buoyant, others, like the blennies and moray eels, lack one and actually 'sit' on the coral. A small hawkfish also props itself between two coral twigs, quietly watching us go swimming past.

Moving fast along the edge of the reef is a hunting school of trevally or horse mackerel, six of them, and a mass of yellow-striped fusiliers race away for refuge in the coral. The reef edge is the hunting place of many larger fishes such as lesser tuna, a number of species of barracuda, trevally and turrum, and big red bass. They patrol great distances of the reef edge, feeding on unwary or isolated fishes, some of them crossing to other reefs.

▷ *A school of yellow-striped fusiliers is silhouetted against the surface as dusk approaches. During the day they live in schools for protection, and hover in the water column off the front edge of reefs where ocean currents are strong and there is a good supply of plankton in the water. As dusk approaches they can quite often be seen feeding actively on the rising plankton before they retire singly, and settle deep into the coral for the night.*

▽ *This school of yellow-tailed fusiliers feeds on plankton. During the day they can be seen patrolling anywhere up to fifty metres off the front of a reef. But as darkness approaches, the schools become tighter, and the fish seek the protection of the reef. As darkness falls, they change colour to a drab blue with a mottled appearance and the belly takes on a reddish tinge. At night they rest motionless deep in caves and among the branches of the coral for protection.*

Yellow-tailed fusiliers, *Caesio cuning*

Sharks drift by

A large shark may drift by off the reef edge – majestic, powerful and very beautiful. A sick or disabled fish sends out unusual swimming 'signals' and if these are picked up by the sensitive pressure receptors of the shark the fish is chased and eaten immediately.

Attacks by sharks on swimmers and divers on the reef are rare and the sharks we see may be curious, but are usually timid. Occasionally, territorial sharks may be aggressive. A rush by a grey reef shark seems more a warning than an attack, but all sharks should be treated with care. Unpredictable, and potentially dangerous, they sometimes become too curious, but they seldom affect the enjoyment of diving in the waters of the Great Barrier Reef.

The shark's eye seems particularly adapted to dim light, and most sharks are active at dusk and after dark. They also have pressure sensitive pores on the

Yellow-striped fusiliers, *Caesio chrysozonus*

Trevally, *Caranx melampygus*

White-tipped reef shark, *Triaenodon obesus*

Trevally, *Caranx sexfasciatus*

Whaler shark, *Carcharinus*

△ *The six-banded trevally is said to reach a weight of 40 kilograms or more. Here a school of young trevally search for small fishes along the reef base.*

△△ *Big trevally hunt the edge of the reef during the daylight hours, but seem most active at dawn and dusk. Here a blue trevally drifts past two pennant coral fish off the edge of the reef.*

'There is tension at dawn and dusk, when large swift-swimming fishes appear out of the gloom.'

body and any unusual movements in the water around them are sensed. They have little difficulty in picking up the movement of a prey, and can also sense its direction. A shark with covered eyes has still been able to catch prey in an experimental tank. In the dark of night a shark will both sense and see a diver long before the diver even becomes aware of the shark.

A fish hooked on the reef by an angler after dark is often immediately pounced on by a shark, suggesting that those canny scavengers are actively searching in the dusk for disabled fishes sending out unusual swimming signals. Divers often see sharks at night by torchlight, but aggression towards humans seems to be extremely rare. Sometimes a small-toothed shagreen or tawny shark, two to three metres long, may be seen over the reefs, showing two large equal-sized fins clear of the water in front of the tail fin. It is not known to attack man.

△ *Sleek and streamlined, big sharks drift effortlessly along the reef. Sometimes they seem timid and flee from divers, but often they ignore them, moving majestically by, as though aware that they have few effective enemies. There are many species of shark on the reef and one of them, the whaler shark, can be fiercely aggressive to divers. Threatening behaviour includes hunching of the back, and rapid opening and shutting of the mouth, which may occur before an attack.*

△△ *The white-tipped reef shark is a common sight off the edge of the reef and over coral beds and seems to live in one area, occupying a territory. It is not usually aggressive and seldom exceeds one and a half metres in length.*

Oval spot butterfly fish, *Chaetodon speculum*

Blue-patch butterfly fish, *Chaetodon plebeius*

Blue-spotted boxfish, *Ostracion cubicus*

△ The beautiful, small blue-patch butterfly fish is abundant on most reefs in sheltered areas of living coral. Blue-patches are easy to approach underwater and are not alarmed by divers.

△△ The oval spot butterfly fish has a very distinct false eye spot. It is thought that this false eye makes a predatory fish strike incorrectly, with the fish swimming off in the 'wrong' direction. The true eye is concealed by a dark bar. There have been many theories as to why coral reef species are so colourful. One of the more likely explanations is that individuals within a species can more easily recognise their own kind from among the bewildering array of similarly shaped fishes.

Carnival time

The sun is now higher and the colours show to their best advantage. So many fishes are swimming above and around the coral that the reef is gay with colour and movement. It has a carnival atmosphere. The butterfly fish, true pierrots of the reef, move merrily over the living coral, taking small nips of coral flesh as they move from shrub to shrub. If we watch them for some time, we can see that they are following a pattern. They travel over roughly the same path, never taking too much from any one coral clump, and cover a 'home range', an area of a few metres for some species, a hundred metres or more for larger butterfly fish. They know these areas in minute detail – the best feeding spots and every coral channel, shelter hole and crevice in which to hide.

   If you are dangerous you do not need to hide. Fire fish and some poisonous puffers flaunt bright

△ This little boxfish releases a poisonous mucus from its skin and is distasteful for predators. It swims using its side fins and often tucks its tail to one side. Boxfish are common on coral and mainland reefs. The juvenile form is bright yellow with black spots.

▷ Striped butterfly fish move over the coral, taking small nips at coral polyps. They usually cover a fairly wide area, but other species may defend a small territory and they often travel over roughly the same path. These magnificent fish are common on coral reefs, especially on the upper slopes and near the reef edge.

Striped butterfly fish, *Chaetodon trifasciatus*

Staghorn coral, *Acropora nobilis*

△ *When the gloominess of the early morning has gone, the reef is friendly and colourful and numerous small fishes can be seen swimming over the coral. Most of the zooplankton leave the surface at this time of day and move just above the sea bottom or even in the sand. As a result the water is dazzlingly clear – sunlight is able to penetrate to greater depths, and visibility is good.*

warning colours which say, 'You have touched me once and it was unpleasant, don't you remember?' The comical little boxfish swims by, using only its side fins like a paddle-wheeler. The skin exudes an unpleasant mucus, making it fairly safe from attack.

A friendly reef

Most of the plankton have left the surface, some species swimming just above the sea bed sand, or even burrowing in it. Many are in the coral crannies, and the open-sea species are many metres deep. With sparse zooplankton and the sparkling sunlight, visibility is very good and the reef seems bright and friendly.

The tension of dawn and dusk, when big fishes appear out of the gloom, is over. The diver, and perhaps the fishes, feel safer at this time and the corals show their soft colours to best advantage. They have drawn in their dart-filled tentacles and

closed their polyp mouths because they feed when the rich night plankton cover the reef, and may now be digesting plankton caught during the previous night. The small symbiotic plants, zooxanthellae, in the corals' cells are rapidly making food, using the sun's energy by the chemical process called photosynthesis. Some of this food 'leaks' to the corals. Larger algae and algal turf also use the sun's energy to make food and to grow, and the water over the lagoon bubbles with oxygen, a by-product of photosynthetic food production.

Many reef animals, including some sponges, sea squirts and molluscs, have come to a useful arrangement with zooxanthellae during evolution. The giant clams expose their beautifully coloured and patterned fleshy lips, filled with algae, to the sunlight, supplementing their plankton diet from the constant stream of water they filter. As we swim slowly over one, it convulsively jerks its two shells;

'In its mantle the giant clam has sensitive eyes that respond to shadows. It is a fully protected species, which grows to a great size.'

◁ *The giant clam is said to weigh up to 260 kilograms, and to reach a hoary age of hundreds of years. It is open to the sun during the day, and the minute algae in its lips produce carbohydrates using the sun's energy, and provide some of the clam's food. Water passes through its mantle, providing oxygen and plankton.*

▽ *In the noon sun the colours of the corals are at their best showing delicate blues, mauves, pinks, yellows and fawns. The combination of the colours and their varied shapes of turrets, plates, delicate shrubs and solid boulders makes magical underwater landscapes.*

Giant clam, *Tridacna gigas*

Corals

Grey-and-white puller, *Acanthochromis polyacanthus*

Swimming in the shallows

'When two goatfish spar with their barbels it is difficult to tell whether they are males fighting or a pair fondling each other.'

◁ ◁ *Grey-and-white pullers are very common in the lagoon. They seem to be the only species that cares for both eggs and young. During the day they are all out seeking plankton above the coral, but at dusk the parents will chase the young down into the coral to sleep.*

◁ *The harlequin tuskfish, one of the wrasses, is common all over the reef. It is easy to pick out with its brilliant colouring as it searches the lagoon floor for crustaceans and molluscs.*

Harlequin tuskfish, *Choerodon fasciatus*

Anemone fish, *Amphiprion perideraion*

△ *Anemone fish are only found with large anemones and seem immune to the batteries of stinging cells in their tentacles, although other small fishes will die if they strike the anemone. But it seems that when an anemone fish first settles it is not totally immune, and will touch the anemone, move away, and repeat this performance many times, apparently slowly building up resistance, probably by covering itself with mucus from the anemone, until it is unaffected.*

◁ *Below the chin, bicolour goatfish have very sensitive barbels that can be folded away in a groove or brought forward to use for tasting. Goatfish often follow other larger fishes digging and blowing on the lagoon floor, sweeping the disturbed surface with their barbels and sensing small edible items, such as small animals missed by the larger fishes.*

Bicolour goatfish, *Parupeneus barberinus*

Damselfish

Coral cod, *Cephalopholis miniatus*

it has small eyes that respond to our shadows and are probably necessary to save its exposed flesh from hungry fishes.

Activity at its highest

The water has risen high enough for the grazers to swim over the reef edge into the shallow lagoon, and we can comfortably follow. The day activity is at its highest. A tuskfish is digging on the lagoon floor, followed by a goatfish that wriggles its two chin bristles across the turned-over sand to sense tasty morsels too small for the tuskfish. Clouds of damselfish are above every coral shrub, feeding on the sparse day plankton, and a pair of anemone fish plough into the protective tentacles of their anemone as we come close.

The one species of fish that carefully guards its young, the grey-and-white puller or spotty-tail, is common here. A pair of adults watch over their swarm of two dozen young, ready to chase off any predator who takes too close an interest, then shepherd their young to the shelter of the coral. The parental drive is strong, and if a swarm of young loses its parents other grey-and-white pullers have been known to add them to their brood.

An object of interest

As we swim over the coral we are not only the observers; we are objects of interest to some fishes and of fear to others. Some of the smaller ones watch and follow, and we attract a swarm of fishes from nearby corals. But the bigger fishes – four large blue surgeonfish and a large Maori wrasse – just drift away. A predatory fish of human size would probably be a threat to the larger fishes but ignore the smaller ones, and they respond accordingly.

If we should sit beside a coral without moving for a long time, the scene would slowly revert to its normal pattern. Aqualungs emit a noisy stream of bubbles every half minute or so, which initially disturbs the fishes. Living underwater in a habitat for two weeks, and using a rebreather that does not emit bubbles, we can get so close to a large bream that its scale rows can be counted to check its identification.

Rest for the night feeders

A small group of spangled emperors, their bodies pale and merging with the sand, drifts past in a lagoon channel beside a coral patch. They will become active at dusk. Many of the other nocturnal species are now taking their rest. In coral caves we can see scores of fifty-millimetre cardinal fish schooling all day in shelter, ready to spread out in mid-water at nightfall. By looking through the entrance to a deep cavern and becoming accustomed to the dim light, we can also see squirrelfish and soldier fish. Both groups are red and almost invisible when they come out to feed at night. The scarlet-fin soldier fish shows a brilliant scarlet dorsal fin as it turns in its cavern.

Scarlet-breasted Maori wrasse, *Cheilinus fasciatus*

◁ △ *Staghorn coral often forms dense thickets in slightly sheltered water. A patch in the lagoon makes an ideal habitat for a myriad of small fishes, providing perfect shelter from large predators. The tiny damsels can easily slip down into the deep recesses of the thicket. The upper portions of the staghorn branches are alive and grow rapidly. The lower portions may be dead and algal-covered, providing food such as worms, molluscs and crustaceans that attracts a mass of different kinds of fishes over the staghorn beds.*

◁ *A number of small species of rock cod live among the corals of the lagoon, pouncing on any dead or disabled fish and feeding on small invertebrates. One of these is the coral cod, an opportunist who takes almost anything it can find. This is the fish most likely to be caught by an angler dangling a bit of fish bait over a coral reef.*

'As a diver swims past, smaller fishes come to investigate and larger ones drift away. A fish of human size would be a threat to larger fishes, but would ignore the smaller ones. They respond accordingly.'

△ *The scarlet-breasted Maori wrasse is a relative of the harlequin tuskfish and is widespread over the reefs of the Pacific and Indian oceans though it does not reach Hawaii. It is common in the lagoon and grows to about a third of a metre in length, unlike its close relative the giant wrasse which reaches over two metres and weighs about 200 kilograms.*

Leopard sea cucumber, *Bohadschia argus*

Textile cone, *Conus textile*

Crown-of-thorns starfish, *Acanthaster planci*

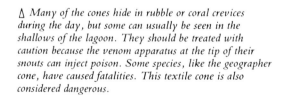

Spider shell, *Lambis lambis*

△ Many of the cones hide in rubble or coral crevices during the day, but some can usually be seen in the shallows of the lagoon. They should be treated with caution because the venom apparatus at the tip of their snouts can inject poison. Some species, like the geographer cone, have caused fatalities. This textile cone is also considered dangerous.

△△ Sea cucumbers are common on the lagoon floor. The leopard sea cucumber is one of the most striking in colour, and the most common is the black sea cucumber, an almost inert form of life 200 to 300 millimetres long. Lying in hundreds in the lagoon, they are very slow growing. Oral tentacles sweep the surface for food particles and sand that are passed to the mouth and through the body. They seem to be safe from predators and, if threatened, exude sticky, toxin-containing threads.

△ It is common in many lagoons to find a few crown-of-thorns starfish and to see where one has fed on a coral. The crown-of-thorns feeds by turning its stomach outwards, pressing it against the coral and digesting it. When, the next morning, the stomach is withdrawn and the starfish moves under the coral for daytime shelter, a round, white, dead patch of coral is left.

◁ The spider shell is a large and colourful shell quite common in the lagoon. Unlike many molluscs, spider shells do not hide during the day and are often seen in the shallows. This one has been turned over to show its lovely colouring. It has eyes on long stalks and a strong and mobile foot, tipped with a hard horny end, with which it moves. The horny tip is stuck into the sea bed just ahead of the shell, and pulled down and back, lifting the whole shell, which falls forward a few millimetres as the foot gets past the balancing point. Primarily herbivores, they are also scavengers.

On the lagoon floor

'The sea cucumber and blue sea star seem immune to predation while the crown-of-thorns starfish is the most notorious predator of the reef. All are echinoderms.'

◁ *A few stony corals, such as this one, have their polyps out and feeding during the day. It is fairly common in lagoons, and there are colonies of about 300 millimetres across, although it grows to three or four times this size. With its stinging cells it feeds on plankton. But it is quite safe for humans to touch the soft polyps, which draw back into the solid skeleton for safety.*

Stony coral, *Montipora*

Slate pencil urchin, *Heterocentrotus mammilatus*

△ *The slate pencil urchin is not very common and is rarely seen. It is not known what its long and very strong spines are for – perhaps they provide protection through strength, for it is certainly difficult to pull one out of the coral if it is wedged in by its spines. Some islanders thread them to make necklaces.*

◁ *The blue sea star is one of a number of sea stars on the reef, but because of its abundance and distinctive colour it is one of the easiest to see. Like the sea cucumbers this species seems to be immune to predation and lies in the open. Perhaps it is distasteful to hungry fishes.*

Blue sea star, *Linckia laevigata*

Black-tipped reef shark, *Carcharinus melanopterus*

△ *The black-tipped reef shark is one of the most common sharks in shallow water over the coral and fortunately is harmless to man. This pair, which are hunting just behind the reef crest, are likely to race off in fear if they are disturbed.*

A prickly plague

We see a white patch of dead coral the size of a soup plate, and know that a crown-of-thorns starfish must be close by. It is found after a few minutes' search under coral ledges, but is left untouched because its spines are sharp and covered with an irritant mucus that will cause pain and then itchiness for a week. When there are only a few, as on this reef, the crown-of-thorns feed by night and hide by day. But when they build up to the huge numbers that have been seen in some areas of the reef over the past twenty years, they feed actively during the

day as well and can be seen in great masses on the coral in the bright sun, looking like a brown and prickly plague.

Life in the shallows

Black sea cucumbers lie everywhere in the warm water of the lagoon shallows and in reef-flat pools, spending their lives passing surface sand through their gut and absorbing food from it. Some of the molluscs are also out in the day. The ring-shaped, annular cowry is common in the shallow water, as is its close relative, the money cowry. We can also see the big common spider shell with its seven large spines, deep red colouring on its underside, and strange habit (common to all its relatives in the Strombidae family) of moving by lifting itself with its horny-tipped foot and falling forwards a few millimetres or so. Other non-spined strombus – the red-mouthed stromb and the flower stromb – lie in

the open in the shallows, as do many of the cones. Beware, some of these cones are very poisonous. Most of the molluscs, however, are not visible. We shall see many of them at night, but now they are under rocks or in coral.

Most of the corals, both hard and soft, withdraw their tentacles and close their polyps during the day but there are species open in the sunlight. One of the very few hard corals open is called *Goniopora*, and if we smooth our fingers across its waving tentacles it steadily withdraws into its skeleton.

Some of the soft corals use their tentacles to grab continuously, like small hands. We pass by the fire coral, or fire weed, with caution, because even the brush of an ankle, exposed between wet suit and flipper, against the creature's feathery fronds, can be painful and cause irritation. It is wise not to scrape corals of any kind, for many will remind you of it for the next few days, and deeper cuts often fester.

'The tenseness of 20th century living ebbs when looking over the pale green sea and feeling at one with the great rhythms of the sun, the moon and the winds.'

Noon on the reef

As we swim slowly back to the boat, two small black-tipped reef sharks swim towards us. They can be fierce predators to the reef fishes, and we have seen a pair chase a school of fishes to a small sandy beach and strand themselves as they rushed the school. But they were unconcerned by the beaching, flapping from side to side in strong swings and slowly working down the wet sloping sand till the next surge caught them. They then herded the school for further attacks. They are harmless to us and fun to watch as they lazily and sinuously swim in our direction, not yet seeing us. When one spots us, in a panic the two turn and rush away.

At noon the colours are bright, but there is markedly less activity. The urgency of feeding seems to have decreased, and the large predators are swimming more languidly. The reef is in a restful mood.

△ *On the island in the noonday sun, life is still. Few birds sing and the reptiles have crept into the shade. It is time to relax in the heat of the day, for animals both above and below the water. In the deep shade of the rainforest patches lovely butterflies still flit about, but even here there is a feeling of a slowing of time. A peaceful world seems content to wait for the noon sun to ease, and then resume the daily battle for existence.*

The reef at night

There is real excitement about a night dive, perhaps because there is a touch of danger. A large shark might not be seen before it strikes, and though thousands of daylight swims and dives have been made safely, the number of night swims attempted is far less. But as yet no one has been harmed. Night diving is also exciting because the search through coral holes and caves, finding sleeping fishes and lovely cowries, is a bit like a treasure hunt.

When studying the night behaviour of certain fishes, an observant colleague with good night vision said that on each dive he saw small reef sharks behind us, a few metres beyond our feet. In a dozen dives we did not see a single shark. We found it more comfortable to concentrate on the fish we were watching and not look back at our legs on the sand behind us.

The changeover begins

At five in the afternoon we take the boat to the spot where we made our morning dive to watch that last hour of light and see the great changeover of the day to the night shift. As we sink down in the water the light is already soft, and the changeover has begun. This is a confused time, and the reef edge predators seem to profit from the confusion. The big trevallies and mackerel are feeding energetically, and every ten minutes or so one or two come racing along the reef, setting up a scurry for shelter among the reef residents with audible thumps made by the power of the tails of the larger species as they take off in fright. Many species are now entering the coral as the light fades. A pair of spotty tails chase their reluctant young down into a coral. A school of small damsels is now nestling among the twigs of an *Acropora*, and the coral is alive with them.

The butterfly fish are disappearing, and one blue-patch butterfly fish is going to sleep in the same branch of coral that it used when we were here last year. When the fish was small the branched coral offered some protection; now it has grown and lies in the fork with its head out at one end and most of the rest of its body out of the other, no longer protected.

The big school of hussars is disappearing, one by one, and we shall find them later, singly working over every metre of the reef. The parrotfish are moving slowly about and entering the coral; the coral trout have gone. With all these fishes now in shelter the scene at dusk has a deserted feeling. Looking up we can see a school of ten or so drummers outlined against the last light in the sky – they are plant feeders, and have come back to rest from their day's foraging. All the fish vegetarians are day workers, although many of the invertebrates prefer to graze at night.

△ *Sunsets from the lagoon can be spectacular, with richly coloured clouds over the mainland. At this time, the nocturnal feeders come out from their daytime hiding places and begin to feed. This is also the time of maximum activity for the plankton, on which many of these creatures feed.*

▷ *Under a flashlight in the last light of day a number of species of small damselfish are beginning to settle into the coral for their night's sleep. This coral is their home, and during the day they forage away from it, but usually only for a metre or so. At night they nestle inside its twigs and seem quite safe from predators. Damselfish are perhaps the most abundant small fishes on the reef.*

Damselfish

Sea urchin, *Diadema setosa*

◁ *Long-spined sea urchins with their needle-sharp spines would seem to have no fear of being preyed upon, but this is not true. Some triggerfish feed on them, and are not deterred by being pierced around the mouth by spines. Perhaps because of this the sea urchin often stays under corals during the day, where the moving spines can often be seen pointing out of a crevice. At night they move in the open, scraping the surface with their sharp beaks.*

▽ *Some of the most beautiful molluscs feed at night, and often the colours and patterns on their bodies rival those on their shells. The cowries are particularly beautiful and their shells are among the most popular in the world. There are many different shaped and coloured cowries, including this tiger cowry.*

Baler shell, *Melo amphora*

Tiger cowry, *Cypraea tigris*

The black-spined sea urchin moves actively about, and many molluscs slide out of shelter or, like the creepers on the lagoon floor, emerge from the sand and feed over the surface. The huge baler shell, a giant mollusc with a foot over six hundred millimetres long, ploughs its way out of the sheltering sand to feed, and if we are lucky we may also find a massive helmet shell. This species also buries itself but often leaves just the tip of the strong shell exposed in daylight, and the result is a little green cap of algae that manage to grow there. The thickness of these tips makes it quite safe from even the strongest toothed wrasse.

The reef by torchlight

Now it is time to use the torch because we can no longer see detail. The beam shows a sight that is always fascinating: a small school of shrimp fish swims head down among the black spines of a

△ *A giant among molluscs, the baler shell has a body and foot growing to 600 millimetres in length. At night the underwater animal world changes and many creatures are out that are not seen by day. Some are small, but some, like the baler shell, are large and conspicuous. During the day the baler buries in the sandy lagoon floor and in daylight it is rare and delightful to find the large majestic mollusc steadily moving over the lagoon floor. The night diver has a chance to see balers searching over the sand for the molluscs that they prey on.*

▷ *On the base of the reef the feather stars are catching their nightly plankton. Most species are on the coral slope, but one feather star is out on the sand, squatting firmly on its long arms by bending some of them to form 'elbows'. The arms use a poisonous mucus to trap drifting plankton that are then passed down food grooves on the upper surface of the arms to a central mouth.*

Feather star, *Comatula rotolaria*

Scorpion fish, *Scorpaenopsis venosa*

▷ *This scorpion fish is out on the coral at night, and presumably is waiting to catch one of the small cardinal fish that are feeding in the water column or any other delectable shrimp or fish that comes its way. Some of this family catch their prey by day, but the majority seem to be nocturnal. As with most fishes, however, little is known of the detail of their daily lives.*

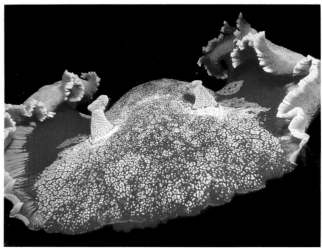

Spanish dancer, *Hexabranchus sanguineus*

△ *This beauty can sometimes be seen in the day, but it is more active at night. The Spanish dancer is a mollusc with brilliant colouring and the ability to swim by making strange undulations of the body. It has also been called, very appropriately, the 'magic carpet'.*

▷ *A nudibranch (meaning 'naked gilled') mollusc is caught by the camera as it moves over the coral at night. This group has scores of species with lovely colour patterns, and there are many species still undescribed. 'Sea slug' is a popular name for nudibranch, a name that does not do justice to the splendid appearance of this green-spotted creature.*

Green-spotted nudibranch, *Nembrotha nigerrima*

'Night diving is rather like a treasure hunt, searching through coral holes and caves, finding jewel-bright molluscs and glimmering fishes. Many species, such as the butterfly fish, have different day and night colour patterns, usually adding spots or blotches at night.'

▽ *The quaint little shrimp fish swims head down, moving around at night. It is found in the long-spined sea urchin where it is well camouflaged with its transparent body and black stripe. Here shrimp fish are in the coral, feeding on small crustaceans from the sea bed. The shrimp fish is encased in a hard transparent box, wafer-thin, elongate, with a tubular snout, and swimming on its head: yet it is superbly adapted to existing successfully in its own particular way on a coral reef.*

Red-backed cardinal fish, *Archamia fucata*; blue-striped cardinal fish, *Apogon cyanosoma*

Shrimp fish, *Aeoliscus strigatus*; coral, *Porites cylindrica*

sea urchin. The shrimp fish is a strange creature: as thin as a wafer, only twenty millimetres deep, and a hundred and twenty millimetres long, seemingly made of transparent plastic, with a black stripe down each side. An extraordinary fish, but when swimming in its usual head-down position between the long black needle-sharp spines of a sea urchin, it is both beautifully camouflaged and well protected by the waving spines. Our torches find an eyed cowry, large and beautifully coloured with bright red rings. Why should a nocturnal mollusc – that covers beauty with its mantle during the day – display such a wonderful and seemingly useless pattern to the dark night? The colouring must have a significance we have not discovered.

Clawed crabs are also about, seeking molluscs. They are unlikely to be able to attack shells the size of an eyed cowry, but are quite capable of breaking open strong shells of smaller size.

△ *Two species of cardinal fish school in a coral cavern, awaiting the darkness before moving out to feed. The cardinal fish take over the damsels' daytime role, moving out from their day shelter deep in coral caverns to hunt little planktonic animals in the water above the reef. Unlike the damselfish, cardinals do not stay in schools near the sheltering coral. Instead, they move out, protected by darkness and their own ruddy colouring.*

Squid

Cuttlefish, *Sepia* sp.

Cuttlefish, *Sepia* sp.

△ Distinctive colouring marks this young squid, but like its relative, the octopus, it is able to change colour rapidly. Large elastic cells contain coloured material and when at rest the coloured fluid is concentrated in a small spot. Around and attached to the cells is a series of small muscles which can pull the cell flat, spreading the colour out and making it much more visible. The result can be spectacular, and an excited squid can send waves of blue, gold, russet and many other colours flushing swiftly across its body.

△ ▷ Cuttlefish are not fish at all but molluscs, related to the squid and octopus. They are active over the reef all day long and hunt for prey in the waters off the reef at night. They have excellent vision with eyes very similar in structure to human eyes, and a fantastic ability to change colour to camouflage themselves. Not satisfied with good vision, speed and the ability to change colour, this creature also practises trickery, or 'sleight of hand'. When threatened by a predator, it may suddenly go very dark, then eject a blob of ink into the water which takes a similar shape to its body. The cuttlefish then goes light in colour and swims off rapidly leaving the predator to lunge unsuccessfully at the 'blob'.

△ ▷ ▷ A school of cuttlefish stays just long enough to give us a questioning look, then decides we are too large, or too uninteresting, and shifts off in high gear. These fast-swimming predators use jet propulsion and are very effective at catching fishes moving through the water.

▷ Soldier fish, unlike their gentler cousins the squirrelfish, have a strong spine at the bottom of the gill cover. Handle with care if you ever catch one. This species has a blood-red colouring and strong white markings that help to disguise its shape. Red is not easily seen in the water as water filters out the red end of the light spectrum. Presumably the red colouring of the soldier fish would then look black and be good camouflage in the dark of night.

Soldier fish, *Adiorax ruber*

Squirrelfish, *Myripristis vittatus*

Squirrelfish, *Myripristis*

△ The squirrelfish and the soldier fish are true members of the night shift. They are sturdy spiny fish, invariably red in colour, that school secretively in caverns during the day but come out to feed at night. This pretty squirrelfish, 200 millimetres long, is a common sight during a night dive on the reef.

◁ A school of two species of squirrelfish at the mouth of their cavern at dusk, just before they take the plunge into the hazardous outside world to feed through the night. There are at least 13 species of squirrelfish in Australian waters.

Members of the night shift

'Even at night all shades of the colour spectrum are shown by the reef fishes. Some also change their marking.'

Rare sights and fatal arms

'Feeding on plankton are the corals, whose many small mouths surrounded by tentacles wait for the tiny drifters to touch them and be rapidly impaled.'

Mushroom coral, *Fungia*

▷ *Strange bulb-like tentacles of a mushroom coral out at night. The mushroom coral is a single, very large polyp that as an adult lies loose on the surface. Here it waits for some worm, or other small nocturnal creature, to touch the tentacles, whose groups of coiled stinging cells will instantly pierce and poison the prey. The mushroom coral is always found with tentacles extended. When picked up it will still display its tentacles.*

▷ *The tentacles of this coral are out and ready for action. They have been successful in catching and paralysing two small red bristle worms.*

▽ *A school of flashlight fish, below, below centre and below right, is one of the rarest sights for night divers. This amazing fish has a light organ under the eye, which is a large gland made of parallel tubes that contain luminous bacteria. The bacteria get their food from the fish, and in return give it light. Muscles can turn the light organ down into a black-lined pocket and the light is switched on and off, every five or ten seconds. The light is important for recognition of the individuals of the school, but it also may be used for seeing food.*

Hard coral, *Symphyllia*

Flashlight fish, *Anomalops katoptron*

Flashlight fish, *Anomalops katoptron*

Flashlight fish, *Anomalops katoptron*

Soft tree coral, *Dendronephthya*

Hard coral, *Porites*

Coral and feather star

△ *Fully distended, a colony of soft coral, which lacks zooxanthellae, fully extends its polyp tentacles in order to optimise its chances of capturing planktonic food. White skeletal elements called sclerites are clearly seen in the transparent surface tissue, while red sclerites colour the contrasting polyps.*

◁ *It has been said that the reef at night is just one mass of waiting mouths and, it could be added, a bed of waving fatal arms. The tentacles of corals and the outspread arms of a feather star compete for the tiny swimming and drifting creatures of the night.*

◁◁ *The colonial corals may have very different-sized polyps. The polyps of this coral are small and, although it is feeding and its polyps and their tentacles are expanded, it looks similar to its daytime appearance.*

Soft coral, *Metalcyonium*

Hard coral, *Tubastraed aurea*

△ *Feathery tentacles surround the soft coral's mouth, each with stinging cells to paralyse small zooplankton drifting or swimming in the dark. Expanded in the dark to long, delicate tubes, these polyps will withdraw in daylight.*

▷ △ *The polyps of this coral expand considerably and have several rings of tentacles. Reef overhangs are a typical spot for a coral colony of this type, as well as caves and other sheltered locations.*

▷ *This hard coral often grows in huge domes in sandy situations. The polyps are extremely large and each one has a separate mouth.*

Hard coral, *Goniastrea*

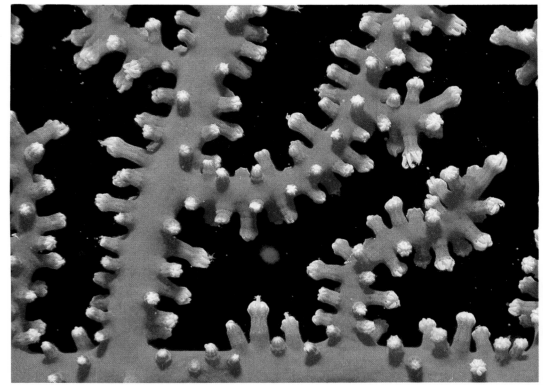

Sea fan, Gorgonian

Expanded polyp mouths

'Night-time plankton pour in hundreds of thousands from the reef crevices, the sandy floor and the deeper water off the reef. This is the time that the coral polyps feed on the rich banquet nature provides.'

Sea fan, Gorgonian

△ Sea fans usually grow at right angles to the current, and here one grows out of the reef face with polyps expanded. The tentacles of the polyps almost touch each other across the spaces, and any small drifting creature has little hope of passing through without getting caught.

◁ The expanded polyps of a sea fan have feathery tentacles with stinging cells, left. Touching the stem of a sea fan causes the polyps to retract, above left, showing the red surface of the stalk.

Sea fan, Gorgonian

'The liveliest and rarest of shells come out to feed at night, better protected then than during the day but still sought by nocturnal predators.'

▷ *A reef crinoid, more like an exotic crimson plant than an animal, is often prominently located, showing a bewildering array of brilliant colour patterns. Feather stars generally select sites that provide a good flow of water because they are passive suspension feeders, filtering minute plankton from the current.*

Feather star, *Himerometra robustipinna*

Feather stars

△ *Although feather stars may be seen during the day, many hide in the coral. At night they are much more obvious, moving to prominent positions and holding up their feathery arms to make their nightly catch. Many species are revealed in the torch light, and some of them have very varied colouring. The reason for this phenomenon is not known.*

▷ *Basket stars impale their prey on tiny hooks on the undersides of their arms. The stars feed on fish and crustacean larvae, shrimps and worms. From time to time, the catch is transferred to the mouth by scraping the entire arm over comb-like oral spines. Remaining hidden during the day, this basket star will mount the same exposed perch to feed each night.*

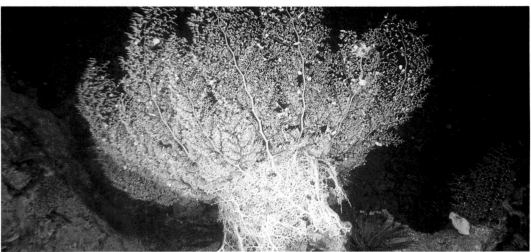

Basket star, *Astroboa*

As we shine the torch beam into the water its rays are reflected by small silvery cardinal fish that have left their caves and have spread out to feed on the mass of night-time plankton that has poured in hundreds of thousands from the reef crevices, the sandy floor and the deeper water off the reef. The cardinal fish replace the damsels of the day, but unlike them do not stay in schools near sheltering coral. Instead they move boldly out, protected by the darkness and their pink or red colouring.

Also feeding on the plankton are the corals themselves, many small mouths surrounded by tentacles, waiting for the tiny drifters, perhaps a worm or crustacean, to touch them and be rapidly impaled by the stinging darts that the corals, jellyfish and their relatives use to such effect. Other plankton feeders are also netting this harvest. A big basket star has climbed up a whip coral and is spread out against the current, a living plankton net. Scores of feather stars have their complex 'feathers' held up above the coral, also sifting for their nightly plankton meal.

Every now and then a larger fish flits over the sand at the base of the coral, chasing the molluscs, shrimps and crabs that feed on the sandy slope. Among these are many of the hussars, sweetlips and sea bream, as well as a huge trevally. If we search now behind the reef crest, on the reef flat and lagoon, we will see many of the liveliest and rarest of shells. Cowries, olives, volutes and mitres come out to feed, better protected at night than during the day, but still sought by the nocturnal predator.

The day-feeders rest

We are engrossed by the holes and caverns in the coral, for here all the fishes that we saw during the day are resting, and many of them are so sleepy that we can pick them up in our hands. Under a ledge is a big coral trout that moves slowly away from the torch beam, bumping the coral. But as we reach out and touch it, the trout suddenly takes off, wildly blundering past. We are always very careful of unicorn fish for their long spike is hard, and a large

▷ △ *Rare and beautiful molluscs are out at night. Spindle cowries feed on soft corals, and may be coloured to match their hosts, thus avoiding becoming prey themselves. This spindle cowry has the colour of its sea fan, and white spots simulating its polyps.*

▷ *A colourful crayfish out on the coral at night. By carefully looking under coral caves and crevices on most reefs, a crayfish, even if only a juvenile, can usually be found. But they are tucked well away. At night they come out to feed, scavenging over the reef. Although they are delicious eating they are too sparsely spread to be the basis of an effective industry.*

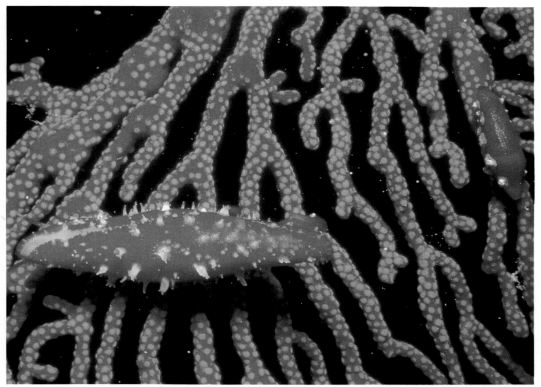

Spindle cowry, *Volva*

Crayfish

▷ *Many of the butterfly fish have different colours for night and day. They are typically day feeders, and at night hide away in the coral, often resting in the same branch of coral or small cave. In the day the little citron butterfly fish is a light yellow, with fine spots and a black stripe camouflaging the eye. But at night, below right, it darkens to a brownish hue, and two strong white blotches appear on its side. Presumably this colouration gives better nocturnal protection.*

▽ *The Moorish idol looks like a different species at night, far below, with its large white central bar blacked out. This makes it more difficult to see.*

Citron butterfly fish, *Chaetodon citrinellus*

Moorish idol, *Zanclus cornutus*

Moorish idol, *Zanclus cornutus*

Citron butterfly fish, *Chaetodon citrinellus*

Chevroned butterfly fish, *Chaetodon trifascialis*

fish could drive its sharp horn into a human chest if it blundered into one in a panic.

Beautiful butterfly fish are now showing their night colours. The right-angled butterfly fish has a dark bar along its body with two brilliant white patches that are not visible in its daytime pattern. Most of the butterfly fish have night patterns differing from those of the day, usually adding spots or blotches. Presumably this breaks up the body shape further and deceives the occasional nocturnal predator such as a large eel. During the day most of the butterfly fish are not territorial, but at night they are, and fight hard over their resting places. A threadfin butterfly fish tried to settle down to a sheltered spot between two coral rocks that it had used previously, only to find it occupied by a small grouper. After swimming in and out of the spot for some time, clearly disconcerted, it swam firmly in front of the grouper, which could have eaten it whole, and then backed into the grouper's head with its sharp anal fin spines erect. The grouper left.

Nocturnal activity

Yellow-striped fusiliers are in many of the crevices. They are no longer in the large schools of the day but are now single, and they have changed colour from blue with distinctive yellow stripes along the body to pink with four or five pale crossbars. They move sluggishly in the beam of light, snuggling deeper into the coral.

We see three large red-and-white-banded shrimps moving in the coral, and one is picking over a small blue-spotted rock cod, taking off parasites. It also feeds on the sea bed, but has in part the role of a nocturnal fish parasite picker.

Among the rock cods the pretty black-spotted barramundi cod always seems to be moving about the corals at night and must be a nocturnal feeder. One rock cod slips away from the light beam through a coral channel.

◁ *At night the chevroned butterfly fish develops a strong black bar running along its body with a pair of dense white patches quite unlike its day colours, above left. This is a fiercely territorial species, unlike many of the other butterfly fish, and guards its coral home, often a platform Acropora coral, against all comers.*

'Camouflage is one reason why the reef fishes are so highly coloured – it is the only way to fit into an environment where the other flora and fauna are far from drab.'

Chevroned butterfly fish, *Chaetodon trifascialis*

The colours of night

'If the base of a sea whip is gently shaken a small goby will probably be disturbed and shoot quickly away.'

▷ At night many anemones close and enfold their commensal anemone fish. Here a pair of anemone fish peep out from their nocturnal home. They are usually found in pairs, with the female larger than the male.

▷ ▽ Some small gobies make their homes on sea whips. This one is almost transparent above, but the lining of the body cavity contains red pigment, helping to camouflage it on its chosen sea whip. They are very difficult to see under water.

▽ Head down in the coral is a vibrantly coloured surgeonfish. It does not change its brilliant colours as it rests through the night. Although this fish is alone, it occurs more often in small schools. It should never be handled as a wound from its caudal blades can be serious.

Anemone fish, *Amphiprion perideraion*

Surgeonfish, *Acanthurus dussumier*

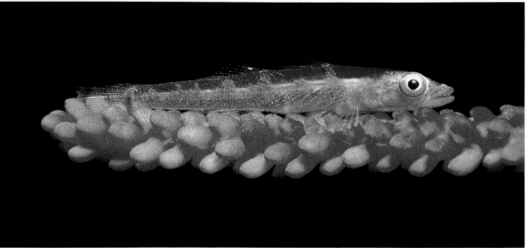

Goby, *Gottogobius yongei*

Blunt-headed parrotfish, *Scarus gibbus*

Blunt-headed parrotfish, *Scarus gibbus*

Fusilier, *Caesio chrysozonus*

Wrasse, *Coris aygula*

△ *A parrotfish, top, lies in its night dress, above, a cover of mucus that it produces each night before sleeping in the coral, perhaps to confuse predators that hunt by smell. It is often so transparent that it can only be seen by the specks of sand that have washed on to it.*

▷ △ *In the coral crannies fusiliers are common. One rests quietly, now pinkish-red with four pale crossbars, no longer the bright blue with two gay yellow stripes of the daytime. And at night it hides singly, not in groups.*

▷ *Awake in the coral is the beautiful young wrasse. The adult of this species loses the red and black spots and is less lovely with its green colour and pale crossbar.*

The blue-spotted stingray is widespread in tropical coral reefs of the Indian and Pacific oceans. On the Great Barrier Reef it is one of the most common rays that the diver sees, and often flits from one coral clump to another in the shallow water of the lagoon during the day. At night it may partially bury itself in the sand. Be careful you do not kneel or stand on it. Its one or two needle-sharp barbs on the tail have a coating of poisonous mucus that can hurt badly.

Blue-spotted stingray, *Taeniura lymna*

Barramundi cod, *Chromileptes altivelis*

Damselfish, *Pomacentrus popei*

△ *The lemon damsel is tucked in among sponges at night, while feather stars feed around it. Damselfish are sometimes found alone but are more frequently seen in groups. They move under the light of a torch and, unlike some fish, do not seem to sleep soundly.*

◁ *The pretty barramundi cod is so often out in the coral at night that it must surely be a night feeder. It is a delicious eating fish, but it is a pity to hunt such a beautiful creature for food. This specimen is a juvenile. The adults are darker and have more numerous spots. Barramundi were once common in northern waters, but commercial fishing has seriously depleted their numbers.*

'So many species live together, each in its own way, in this great structural mass of corals like an underwater city. At times the reef seems so crowded it's like rush hour.'

Banded coral shrimp, *Stenopus hispidus*

Resting and sleeping

We see a sight that never fails to amaze. A large parrotfish, weighing about two kilograms, is lying on its side, completely encased in gelatinous mucus. The coating is so transparent that it is visible only because a thin scatter of sand has stuck to the envelope, showing its outline – an extraordinary habit. Fish of the same species can be found with or without the cover at night, and sometimes with a partial cover. Perhaps its presence prevents the scent of the fish being picked up by a nocturnal predator, some of which, such as certain eels, hunt by smell.

A number of stingrays are now feeding on the sea bed and, while peering into the coral, we must be careful where we put our legs. The most common stingray is the small blue-spotted ray and its sharp tail barbs can be extremely painful.

Although some fishes are asleep in the coral, many seeming to become fully unconscious,

damsels move under the torch beam, as do the butterfly fish, and seem to rest rather than sleep.

As we swim slowly just under the surface, back to the boat, we ponder on the fishes we have seen in the beam of our torches; the few making their living in the night, and the much larger number of species resting in the coral for the activity of tomorrow. The richness of these different forms must surely be partly due to the tremendous capacity of coral to create such extensive reefs, from thousands of small patches to single reefs many kilometres long, all with an infinite variety of shelter places for invertebrates and fishes. The reef is an evolutionary laboratory, in which hundreds of thousands of different species have been developed, tested, and discarded if found wanting, or added to the huge throng of species if successful. But the greatest puzzle is how so many species can find food and shelter, and co-exist in such close communities.□

△ *A pair of banded coral shrimp or cleaner shrimp delicately feeds during the nocturnal round. Small animals are picked from the surface, but the coral shrimp has also developed the specialised role of a nocturnal fish cleaner and can sometimes be seen walking over a sleeping fish, picking off external parasites. Growing up to sixty millimetres long, the shrimps are white with deep red bands across claws, head, abdomen and tail. Each of the long antennae are three-branched and their size is designed to attract customers to their cleaning station.*

Staghorn coral, *Acropora*

Part two: the reef's origins

The Great Barrier Reef is situated off the eastern coast of Queensland, in relatively shallow waters rarely more than 60 metres deep. This is the world's largest coral reef province, and it extends over an area of 230 000 square kilometres from the Gulf of Papua along 2300 kilometres of coastline to just beyond the Tropic of Capricorn. Over 2100 individual reefs make up the main barrier, with a further 540 high continental islands closer inshore having significant fringing reefs.

Single coral reefs may cover an area of over 100 square kilometres; massive structures that have been built almost entirely by marine plants and animals. The material of the reef is calcium carbonate: limestone derived from the surrounding waters by the reef organisms. The living reef forms merely a veneer, adding new limestone to these massive structures at rates that can be annually measured in kilograms for every square metre of the reef surface.

Corals are probably the most obvious life forms of the reefs. Their intricate and colourful shapes are colonial structures made up of thousands of individual polyps, each secreting its small cup of coral limestone. Not surprisingly, until the middle of the 18th century corals were regarded as plants, not animals. However, these flower-like creatures provide the building blocks for reef construction.

Plants are also important in the development of the system, as many secrete limestone. Coralline algae in particular form cementing crusts that act as 'mortar' for the coral 'bricks'. Innumerable other plants and animals also contribute, forming fine sand and coarser skeletal material which ends up as either sediments on the reef surface or as infill in the many cavities that develop within the reef.

Coral reefs have existed in the earth's shallow seas for a long time, probably in excess of 450 million years; a clear indication of how successful a life form they are. Although the original corals, called rugose corals, became extinct about 200 million years ago, the reefs they formed were probably very similar to modern coral reefs. The scleractinian corals that succeeded the rugose forms probably evolved in the warm waters of the Tethys Sea, a massive ancient ocean which originally existed between the northern European and Asian land masses and the southern African and Indian continents. It was eventually closed by the gradual northward migration of the southern continents, a process known as continental drift. The closing of the ancient sea was earliest in the west and latest in the east, so that the evolving corals were slowly pushed eastwards into the shallow peninsulas and island-studded seas of the western Pacific. It is this area which has by far the greatest diversity. Over 500 coral species are known in this region.

At the same time as the Tethys Sea was closing and the modern corals were evolving, the Australian continent was also on the move, slowly drifting northwards from the cold polar latitudes into the warmer waters of the tropics. By chance, its migration took it into this area rich in coral growth. Its northeastern shores in particular were bathed by oceanic waters passing through the coral-rich seas.

The Great Barrier Reef is thus relatively young, having started to grow probably no more than 18 million years ago, with many parts little more than one million years old. However, this was a period of great environmental fluctuation in the earth's history. Sea levels in particular have oscillated from positions slightly higher than present to at least 150 metres below the present level.

Corals and associated life forms were able to survive these massive environmental changes, and this is indicative of how resistant to natural disturbances this ecosystem is. The coral reef has a very high order of internal organisation, greater even than the tropical rainforests of the adjacent humid landmasses, with which coral reefs are frequently compared. Both environments receive high levels of solar radiation, the ultimate source of all ecosystem energy.☐

▽ *The coral formations of the Great Barrier Reef make up the most extensive structure ever built by living creatures. At low tide the reefs extend to the horizon.*

◁ *Hardy staghorn coral thrives in areas with plenty of water movement and sunshine. Many* Acropora *species regenerate from broken pieces.*

Hydroid coral, *Distichopora violacea*

Corals: animal, vegetable or mineral?

The reef builders

Corals are an extraordinary group of animals that provide the framework, both living and dead, of the reef. They are responsible for much of the reef's scenic beauty and provide shelter for its more mobile occupants. Corals are strange, puzzling creatures. With shapes that are solid and unyielding, or soft but firmly attached to the reef, formed into mounds, plates, branches and crusts, they seem more like rocks or plants than animals.

The true nature of corals can best be appreciated if three things are kept in mind. Firstly, they are positioned between sponges and various worm-like groups on what biologists call the 'evolutionary scale'. With jellyfish and sea anemones they belong in the phylum Coelenterata: animals with special prey-catching cells called nematocysts and a simple body plan in which one opening is used for the passage of materials both into and out of the body.

Secondly, and more remarkably, corals are for the most part modular organisms, occurring not as a single animal with a single set of bodily characteristics, but as a special kind of colony. A coral colony is not a group of related individuals living and working together for the common good. Rather, it is the result of a single founder individual dividing to replicate itself over and over again, repeating the set of organs vital for its maintenance and reproduction. This modular characteristic provides corals with an array of special features and abilities. The entity that is the colony has a form of its own, with a base attaching it to the reef, a growing edge zone, an upper surface exposed to the light and a shaded under-surface. It also has hundreds of individual units – the polyps. These are genetically identical and are united by common tissue connections, and as a result are in constant beneficial communication.

The third and most remarkable feature of corals is

◁ *Corals are like an art form with endless variations of shape and wonderful subtleties of colour. Small colonies of the Hydrozoan coral,* Distichopora violacea, *are extremely common, usually in situations sheltered from sunlight. Hydrozoans are more akin to jellyfish than to the true corals,* Scleractinia.

Hard coral, *Favia favus*

Hard coral polyp

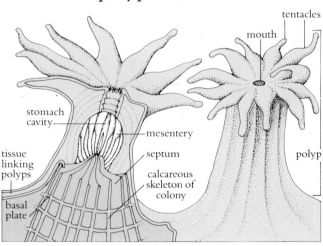

◁ *Within its setting in the modular colony, the coral polyp of* Favia favus, *left and above, displays the simple coelenterate body plan – essentially a cylinder with a ring of tentacles at the top, surrounding an opening that serves as both mouth and anus. Inside, the cylinder is partitioned by sheets of tissue extending inwards from the cylinder wall – the mesenteries. On these, the sex cells ripen each year to produce the eggs and sperm that will give rise to the next generation, so their appearance is constantly changing. The walls of the cylinder have three layers, the middle one being the equivalent of the 'jelly' layer of jellyfish. Cells within the outer layer produce the skeleton, in this case of limestone which, by a complex system of foldings of the coral wall, forms struts or septa extending, like the mesenteries, into the centre of the polyp. The patterns produced by the combination of polyp wall and septa are unique for each species.*

the presence of millions of zooxanthellae – tiny single-celled plants – within the animal's tissues. These obtain nourishment from photosynthesis, where the energy from sunlight is used to convert carbon dioxide and water into carbohydrates and oxygen. The presence of zooxanthellae in the coral colony enhances its capacity to grow and lay down skeleton. Quite a number of corals do not have them and some of these, with no need to live in the light, cling to caves, crevices and the underside surface of boulders.

What's in a name?

Like 'worms', 'shellfish' and 'bugs', the word 'coral' can be applied loosely to a variety of animals. They come from several groups with different kinds of polyps, but corals can also be distinguished by the kinds of skeletons they build.

Soft coral polyp

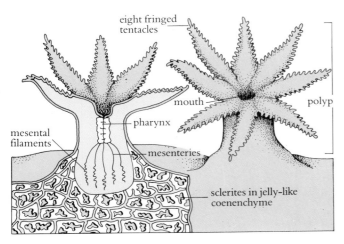

eight fringed tentacles

mouth

polyp

pharynx

mesental filaments

mesenteries

sclerites in jelly-like coenenchyme

Stony coral, *Acropora*

△ Soft corals do not have a solid limestone skeleton. They do, however, have hard parts in the form of tiny limestone crystal structures called sclerites embedded in their tissues. Their polyp structure is similar to that of hard corals, but they have eight fringed tentacles.

▷△ The stony corals are the only animals capable of building massive geological formations. Reaching up to the surface of the ocean, these solid limestone cliffs withstand the buffeting of waves and harness the resources of sunlight and sea to grow ever more solid.

▷ Daisy corals often oblige the daytime diver with an excellent view of expanded polyps. Two rings of smooth tentacles surround the disc with the mouth at its centre. The little yellow dots on the tentacles contain stinging cells for catching prey.

Daisy coral, *Tubastrea*

Daisy coral, *Tubastrea*

Hard coral, *Catalophyllia jardinei*

The strictest use of the term applies to hard corals, which have a white skeleton of limestone (calcium carbonate) and belong to the order Scleractinia, which comprises the 'hard', 'stony' or 'true' corals. These are the creatures that, with the hidden help of their zooxanthellae, create limestone so successfully that they are responsible for the reef's existence.

In contrast to the hard corals, the 'soft' corals, from the order Alcyonacea, appear not to have a skeleton. In fact, they have tiny, hard, elaborate crystalline structures called sclerites in their tissues. These are limestone, but of a different crystal structure from the limestone of stony corals.

Sclerites also occur in another group – the fan and whip corals of the order Gorgonacea – but these animals have a second skeleton which is made of a hard but flexible material called gorgonin, and their appearance differs markedly from that of the soft corals. Sometimes occurring in yellow or orange, with the polyps appearing as tiny, fragile white flowers scattered over the surface, sea fans often live in deeper waters down the face of the reef.

Fringed polyps
Polyps of both these groups (and also a few other small groups) have eight tentacles that are fringed rather than smooth. Corals with this formation of polyps are called octocorals, as distinct from hexacorals, which have smooth tentacles in rings of six and multiples of six.

Soft coral, *Metalcyonium*

△ *The tentacles of hard corals are smooth like those of anemones but their tips may appear knob-like. Those of this hard coral, white with purple knobs, contrast with the brilliant green mouth disc.*

◁△ *When the polyps retract, the daisy coral reveals that it is a stony coral with a hard skeleton. It does not have single-celled plants in its tissues, however, so its brilliant orange colouring does not have the brown veneer that these cells impart.*

◁ *Night falls and this soft coral expands its polyps, their transparent walls revealing the details of their anatomy. The gonads (sex organs) are situated just below the white cylinder of the muscular pharynx. Surrounding the mouth is a crown of eight tentacles fringed with feathery pinnules.*

'Formed into mounds, plates, branches and crusts, corals seem more like rocks or plants than animals.'

Soft coral, *Nepthea*

Soft coral, *Dendronephthya*

△ *Some soft corals have the astonishing habit of wandering about on the reef, extending the tissues in their bases in the direction they wish to travel; not the speediest method of transport, but nevertheless remarkable for a coral colony. Sometimes the dead trails of moving soft corals can be seen on the surface of living hard coral tables. This soft coral has settled on the tip of a colony of black coral,* Cirrhipathes. *Only the skeletons of black corals are actually black or dark brown. Their flesh can be yellow, orange, brown or grey.*

▷△ *The prettiest of the soft corals must surely be* Dendronephthya. *This is because no zooxanthellae mask the brilliant pink, purple and orange sclerites of these translucent colonies.*

▷ *Not all soft corals are beautiful. Some are leathery, dull coloured and lacking in symmetry. Many of these excel at occupying space. The sea squirt in the centre, black with blue tips, has so far repelled the soft coral.*

▷▷ *Like cut-glass miniatures the tiny polyps of an undescribed species of* Dendronephthya *wait patiently for their meal. The minute red sclerites of the polyps are dwarfed by the large white ones which, when the colony is contracted, present a porcupine exterior.*

Soft coral, *Sinularia*

Soft coral, *Dendronephthya*

Soft coral, *Heteroxenia elizabethae*

Soft coral, *Anthelia*

△ *United only by a thin membrane, the tall and relatively large polyps of this soft coral have no body mass into which they can retract. Eager for light, they flourish in unshaded areas and prefer sheltered and shallow parts of the reef.*

△ *Distributed mainly in the surface tissues, the minute oval sclerites of the soft coral family* Xeniidae *diffract the light, giving the colonies an opalescent sheen. This female colony has two types of polyps: the eggs ripen in the polyps shown and tiny ones on the surface of the colony maintain water currents through it.*

The crystal palace

'Soft corals have tiny, hard, elaborate crystal structures in their tissues which are called sclerites.'

Soft coral, *Sinularia flexibilis*

◁ *Species of this soft coral genus have spindle-shaped sclerites, large enough to be seen by the naked eye. These are packed densely into the tissue, and leave behind a kind of skeleton when the coral dies. This material, known as 'spicularite', can form a considerable part of the reef's substance in some inshore reefs where this genus is common. The species vary enormously; this one has extremely soft and flexible snake-like branches that waft to and fro with the water movement.*

'A single coral reef province stretches 2000 kilometres from Capricorn to the low tropics, with reefs of every conceivable shape and size, high islands and low, rough seas and calm.'

▷ *The organ pipe coral has characteristic feather-like polyps that are expanded even during daylight hours. Large and closely arranged, they overlap to cover as much area as possible to catch detritus and other food particles efficiently. Pieces of the strange, bright red, internal skeleton are commonly found in many coarse coral sands. They look like small vertical tubes with cross platforms.*

Organ pipe coral, *Tubipora*

Soft coral, *Sarcophyton trocheliophorum*

Soft coral, *Sarcophyton trocheliophorum*

△ *Many soft corals, in particular the large fleshy forms, are able to alter their external appearance, often with dramatic effect. They achieve this through two processes. If a colony with all of its polyps expanded is gently disturbed, it may partially retract its polyps and immediately alter its appearance. Further disturbance will result in complete retraction of the polyps and a feathery Sarcophyton may take on sharp lines. The main body of the colony, however, is still expanded with sea water, and on further irritation it will gradually deflate. Sarcophyton trocheliophorum excels at this: the fully expanded colony is capable of deflating until portions of the colony pucker into weird contortions.*

▷ *The blue coral is not a true hard coral, but a unique octocoral with no close relatives, placed in a group of its own. When cleaned of its tissues and dried, its skeleton is a beautiful blue, caused by the presence of iron salts. This colour is hidden in the live coral by its dull brown tissues. Blue coral is confined to warm waters, and on the Great Barrier Reef it is an uncommon sight on reefs south of 19 degrees latitude.*

Blue coral, *Heliopora caerulea*

Gorgonian fan coral

Fans and whips

The beautiful fans and whips belong to the Gorgonians group, which also includes the precious red coral from the Mediterranean Sea, as well as various other corals whose dense skeletons are cut and polished or carved into tiny sculptures for coral jewellery. Their solid skeleton is a complex mixture of protein, limestone and minerals. However, most reef Gorgonians do not have this hard skeleton: the protein, sometimes with and sometimes without sclerites, forms a flexible core with a colourful 'skin' surrounding it.

Fans grow at right angles to the current, and when the polyps are expanded their tentacles almost touch, forming a very efficient plankton collector. Some whips form long, unbranched stems, slender and waving in the current. Others are branched, forming bushy tangles to trap food.

Organ pipe coral, *Tubipora musica*

△ *An opportunistic black and white feather star, utilising a tall Gorgonian fan, gets itself up into the food conveying tidal flow away from the eddy currents of the reef surface. The correct generic name of this Gorgonian, often mistakenly called Muricella, is still uncertain.*

◁ *Some of the polyps in this organ pipe coral have withdrawn into their 'pipes', exposing the unmistakable red skeleton. Little pieces of this skeleton are a common sight among the white sands on coral beaches.*

'Corals are carnivores and catch food from the surrounding waters by extending tentacles armed with stinging cells.'

Gorgonian coral, *Ctenocella pectinata*

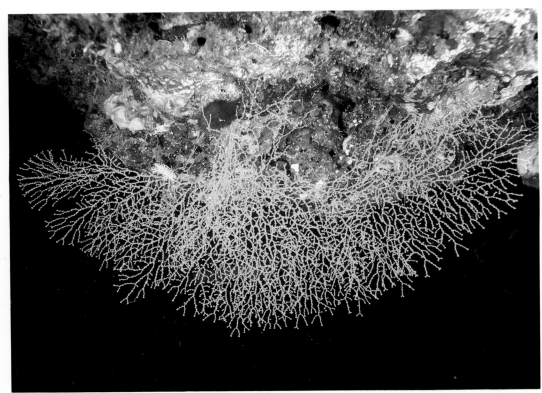

Gorgonian coral, *Acabaria*

△ This Gorgonian coral may incorporate alterations into its geometry as it grows, often with startling, bizarre or even superb results. This ability is the special prerogative of modular organisms.

▷ △ Noted for their bright colours, these Gorgonian coral colonies are commonly found under ledges or attached to cave roofs, indicating possible light avoidance behaviour of the planktonic larvae.

▷ This common Gorgonian is also one of the strongest, belonging to the Holaxian group, which have a continuous axis of hard protein ('gorgonin'). This gives the colony flexibility and strength. The branches are covered by a thick cork-like layer containing lots of zooxanthellae, and it is to the coral's advantage to grow in areas of high light intensity. It is one of the few species of Gorgonians that survives close to the water surface in areas with strong water movement.

Gorgonian coral, *Rumphella aggregata*

Expensive corals

'The Gorgonian whips and fans, and the Antipatharian black corals are beautiful alive, and some are very precious dead.'

◁ *Usually confined to depths below 20 metres, black corals may vary from dense bushy growths to long thin whips. Large, very old colonies are sought for the manufacture of black coral jewellery. A very thin veneer of tissue covers the hard black skeleton, which is adorned with fine thorns. The dense yet flexible nature of the axis, a horn-like material similar to the skeletal axis of Gorgonians, lends itself to shaping and bending and takes a high polish.*

Gorgonian coral, *Subergorgia mollis*

△ *The largest of the reef Gorgonians spreads its net into the current. The strength of the water flow determines the size of the mesh. A floppy fan with a wide mesh taken to a place with stronger currents develops a smaller mesh to give it greater rigidity to cope with its new conditions.*

◁ *In close-up view, a portion of a branch of the black coral whip shows the unusual six-tentacled polyps expanded to capture their prey – the tiny animals which are floating by in the plankton.*

◁◁ *Most Great Barrier Reef Gorgonians are highly coloured, the colour coming from tiny sclerites in the surface tissues which overlay the brown rod of flexible material within. Shades of red and yellow predominate for the sclerites, and different mixing of sclerites allows the spectrum of colony colour to include oranges and rich browns. White, delicate lilacs, pinks and rich purples, however, are not uncommon.*

Black coral, *Antipathes*

Gorgonian coral, *Paramuricea*

Black coral, *Cirrhipathes*

CORALS 69

Fire coral, *Millepora*

Coralliomorph bead coral

△ *The fire coral delivers a burning sting as a sharp reminder of its relationship to the stinging jellyfish. The sting comes from well-loaded nematocyst cells, carried by hollow, mouthless polyps arranged in little circles around a central polyp with a mouth. Fire coral can occur as elegant lacy plates or as sheets and mounds. Divers soon get to know its tell-tale yellow colouring and to remember to wear gloves when diving in the reef front areas that it seems to favour.*

▷ △ *Coralliomorphs are a mysterious little group of anemone-like creatures very closely related to corals but having no skeletons. Their thin, rainbow-coloured discs, covered in clubbed tentacles, are quite often encountered among corals on the reef.*

▷ *Zooanthids are commonly mistaken for soft corals, but they are closer to hard corals. They are colonial, anemone-like animals in which the individual polyps are connected by creeping tubes. These creatures sometimes cover huge tracts of reef flat pavement, and they are very quick to move to parts of the reef that have been cleared of live hard corals.*

Zooanthid; pavement coral

A valuable skeleton

Black coral, from the small subclass Ceriantipatharia, is more familiar in the form of a polished stone than the prickly tree-like formations or corkscrew twists of the live colonies from which it originates. This is because black corals are deep-water animals: even colonies near the bottom of a reef slope do not have the density of skeleton that is prized for cutting and polishing, since the colonies seem only to grow old enough, and hence solid enough, in deeper waters.

Complex hydrozoans

A few coral-like animals belong to the class Hydrozoa, an enormously varied group that includes such animals as the Portuguese man-of-war or bluebottle. These hydrozoan corals are only remotely related to true corals, but they have some characteristics in common with jellyfish.

Their polyps are not divided internally, like the true corals, and individual polyps can specialise in different duties – feeding, defence, reproduction. The feeding polyps have a mouth, but those specialised for defence or prey-catching make no pretence to any function except stinging; these have lots of stinging nematocyst cells, and no mouth. For this reason hydrozoans are to be avoided on the reef.

Hydrozoans live a more complex life than their coral kin. In order to reproduce sexually they must first produce little male or female jellyfish (medusae), which then produce reproductive cells.

Hydroid coral, *Stylaster*

◁ △ *Stylasterines are elegant and sometimes beautifully coloured hydrozoans with hard skeletons. They are sometimes called 'lace corals', which is confusing because this name can also be applied to the bryozoans, animals not remotely related. In* Stylaster, *and also in* Distichophora, *the dead colony skeleton retains the strong colouring.*

◁ *The distinctive fronds of this hydroid deliver a nettle-like sting. The colony contains zooxanthellae and grows much larger than other species of its group, many of which can barely be seen as tiny hairs on the reef waters.*

'Hydroids and fire coral are more closely related to jellyfish than to all the other kinds of coral kin because they produce tiny medusae as the sexual phase in their life cycle.'

Fire coral, *Aglaeophenia cupressina*

Form and pattern

The hard corals have been aptly described as the architects of the reef. The limestone of their skeletons is in the form of needle-shaped crystals that fit together in fan-shaped tufts. These sit one upon another in rods called sclerodermites – the girders that form the basis of the reef's architecture.

Girders placed in different formations give different structures. A basic polyp 'house' has outer walls (theca), floor (basal plate) and internal divisions (septa); sometimes there is also a centre pole (columella).

As the coral colony grows, new polyps are added, either from outside old polyps or from divisions within – sometimes with the formation of common walls. In some corals, when the colony grows, the polyps with their connecting tissues pull upwards and lay down new basal plates, so that a living colony has living tissue and skeleton on top, and untenanted skeleton underneath. The empty skeleton has an architecture that shows the history of the building of the colony.

Reading the plates

The depositing of basal plates is done faster or slower at different times of the year, and in different weather conditions. This gives different densities of basal plates, which show as light and dark bands in the empty skeleton. The age of these corals – like trees – can be ascertained from the calendar of events that occurred during the building process. Some corals on the reef are hundreds of years old, and they carry valuable documentation of meteorological and other events, which scientists are now learning to read.

One enormous polyp

The variety and nature of patterns in hard coral forms is illustrated clearly in mushroom corals, so-named because they resemble overturned mushrooms with the stalks plucked off. A mushroom coral is one huge coral polyp and the skeleton (called a corallite) it has constructed. The dent in its centre is the position of the polyp mouth, and the struts radiating from this are the septa. When the polyp is not withdrawn into its skeleton, dozens of tentacles cover the top of the coral. Unlike most polyps, those of the mushroom coral do not divide and repeat themselves to form colonies.

They are also an exception to another rule in that they do not cement themselves to the reef, but rather live as individuals, unattached to the surface. Very young corals are attached by a stalk that joins the polyp, not where it would on a mushroom, but on the other side, so that the mouth of the polyp is uppermost. When the polyp gets too big for the stalk, it drops off and begins its solitary existence. Mushroom corals usually prefer the quiet waters of pools or lagoons or the deeper water.

Mushroom coral, *Fungia fungites*

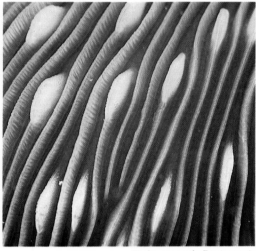

Mushroom coral, *Fungia scutaria*

Mushroom coral, *Diaseris distorta*

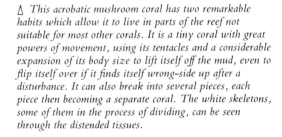

Mushroom coral, *Fungia klunzingeri*

△ *This acrobatic mushroom coral has two remarkable habits which allow it to live in parts of the reef not suitable for most other corals. It is a tiny coral with great powers of movement, using its tentacles and a considerable expansion of its body size to lift itself off the mud, even to flip itself over if it finds itself wrong-side up after a disturbance. It can also break into several pieces, each piece then becoming a separate coral. The white skeletons, some of them in the process of dividing, can be seen through the distended tissues.*

△△ *A big old mushroom coral, one of several species, shows the form that gives the group its common name. They are free-living species found in quieter waters.*

▷ *The extraordinary variety of coral shapes and patterns has intrigued the curious since mankind first walked the coral shore.*

△ *The mushroom corals have enormous skeletons in which the features can be seen easily, above and top, whereas in small polyps a microscope is needed. These skeletons show the structural differences between species.*

Separate walls

When polyps divide, the connections that remain between old and new contain an extension of the stomach cavity, so that nutrients can be passed from one polyp to the next. Even when polyps are well separated by an expanse of skeleton, this connection remains. Many different hard corals have a 'separate but connected' structure. Most of these grow as mounds, but some are sheets, plates or branches. Such corals come from different families and they do not have a uniting common name. The polyps can be very large and easily seen, or so tiny that they cannot be seen without a microscope.

Mushroom coral, *Heliofungia actiniformis*

Acanthastrea echinata

Galaxea astreata

Oxypora lacera

Diploastrea heliopora

Turbinaria peltata

Echinopora lamellosa

Favites chinensis

Brain coral, *Leptoria phrygia*

Turbinaria frondens

Pectinia paeonia

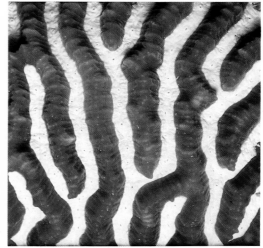

Brain coral, Platygyra daedalea

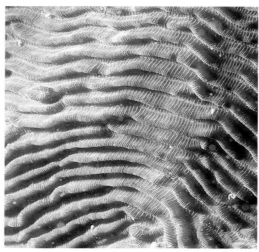

Pachyseris speciosa

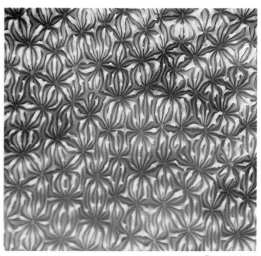

Pavona minuta

'Stony cups, plates, brains and branches
with tapers, ridges, struts and beams,
are different architectural responses to
stress from wave and current, need for
light for the zooxanthellae plant food
factories, and direct competition with
neighbours for space.'

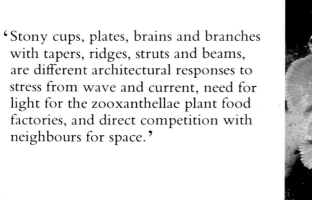

Pectinia lactuca

Pavona decussata

The mighty brains

The fitting common name 'brain coral' belongs to several different species from two families whose colonies look much like the human brain. Long lines are formed by dividing polyps that form walls along their sides but not between their mouths. These colonies are formed in the shape of mounds; they have a thin veneer of living coral over empty skeleton, and all contain internal calendars in the form of light and dark bands.

Some brain corals can be up to two metres in diameter, and have patterns of maze-like intricacy.

Doing their own thing

The coral's modular lifestyle places few limits on the structure of colonies. Some species have drafted blueprints that are unique and sometimes a little bizarre. In these it is sometimes difficult to see where

Pocillopora eydouxi

Brain coral, *Symphyllia radians*

one polyp ends and another begins: walls are eliminated or the centre pole exaggerated; some patterns are streamlined, and some are elaborate.

The branching strategy

In almost every hard coral family there are some branching forms. Branching gives more access to space and allows all the polyps good exposure to the water currents carrying their food. Branching is achieved in various ways, and it has been perfected by corals of the genus *Acropora*. These are the only hard corals known to have two different kinds of polyps (though one kind can change into the other). The first kind – the axial polyp – forms the axis of the branch, and it grows longer and longer, without bothering to pull itself up and lay down basal plates. As it grows, it buds off radial polyps. The axial polyp is a cylinder, but the radials have a distinctive wall structure.

Staghorn coral, *Acropora gemmifera*

Acrhelia horrescens

Needle coral, *Seriatopora hystrix*

Staghorn coral, *Acropora nobilis*

'Branching gives more access to space and allows all the polyps good exposure to the water currents carrying their food. It has been perfected by corals of the genus *Acropora*.'

Staghorn coral, *Acropora tenuis*

◁ *Branching is a common coral form, but there are many variations of the branching habit, from small shrubs with needle-like branches (some* Seriatopora *species) to large thickets two metres high and 50 metres long, with basal branches as thick as a human leg. Growth of branches may be rapid – often 50 to 100 millimetres or more per year. This allows avoidance of competitors for sunlight, or growing clear of a silty lagoon floor. Although branches may break off in violent storms, they often re-grow from the pieces and spread the colony.*

Euphyllia divisa

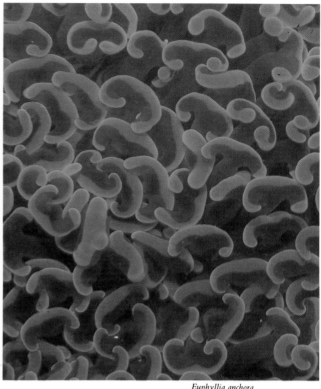

Euphyllia anchora

Hard coral, *Goniopora*

Bubble coral, *Plerogyra sinuosa*

In their true colours

Because hard corals are nocturnal in their habits, the daytime observer sees little more of them than a skeleton with a fine overlay of tissue colour. A few, however, extend their polyps, or at least some part of their surface tissues, during the day, and these offer a different view of hard coral form. While most of the clues to relationships among corals are built into their skeletons (a feature that has led to an excellent fossil record), idiosyncrasies of species or genus are apparent in the tissue; however, these are lost when the coral dies.

△ *The skeletons of these two species of* Euphyllia *are almost identical but their special tentacle shapes separate them immediately. The tentacles of* Euphyllia divisa, *above left, have rounded caps and little branchlets while those of* E. anchora, *above, end in scroll-like expansions.*

◁ *In the daytime, this coral has bubbles of expanded tissue covering a beautifully sculpted skeleton. The tentacles are only expanded during the night, projecting out among the bubbles.*

◁ ◁ *All the polyps of this coral remain continuously extended and these can be many millimetres long. The same phenomenon is seen in its relative,* Alveopora, *which has six tentacles rather than the twelve which are found in* Goniopora.

Sexual reproduction

For a few nights every year, the Great Barrier Reef puts on a spectacular display when corals of many different species, both soft and hard, participate in synchronised mass spawning. Those who have witnessed this spawning describe it as being 'like a fireworks display' or 'an upside-down snowstorm'.

During the months before the event, the gonads (sex organs) of the individual polyps ripen in readiness. The eggs begin their development first, at least six months ahead of time. The testes, with their maturing sperm, usually take less time to ripen. This process is called 'gametogenesis'.

As the sea water warms rapidly in spring, the sex cells also develop rapidly. Eggs become coloured: pink, red or orange, sometimes even purple, blue or green. The sperm in the testes change from simple tadpole-like forms to elegantly shaped heads with long, beating tails. In some corals, the sexes are separate, every polyp in a colony being female or male. More often, the polyps contain both male and female gonads; a condition known as 'hermaphrodite', from the names of the Greek god, Hermes, and the goddess Aphrodite.

On cue with the moon

Once gametogenesis is complete, the corals have only to wait for their cues to spawn. The major cue is provided by the moon. Spawning seems to begin one or two nights after a full moon in late spring or early summer, but activity is greatest on the fourth, fifth or sixth night.

After dusk on the chosen night, the coral colonies ready themselves for spawning. The eggs and/or sperm are gathered beneath the mouths of the polyps. Soon after, the mass is expelled, and the waters above the reef begin to fill with the tiny reproductive cells.

The significance of this occurrence has yet to be explained. For many members of one species to spawn at once ensures a very high rate of cross-fertilisation. Because a coral is fixed and cannot go hunting for a mate, it must cast its seed at the most appropriate time for the maximum production of offspring. However, to do so at a time when the seeds of so many other corals are abroad would seem to involve a great deal of extraordinary confusion.

Synchrony of timing suggests a strong selective advantage, but what can this advantage be? By 'swamping' predators with an over-abundance of food for a short time, a high level of survival is assured. Perhaps the arrival of a night when tidal amplitude is lowest and various other unknown factors are at their most suitable, overwhelms the consideration of bumping into the wrong mate's offspring. Some corals spawn a different way: their eggs are fertilised while still in the polyp, and the polyps brood the developing larvae (called planulae). They are released over long periods.

Staghorn coral, *Acropora*

Staghorn coral, *Acropora formosa*

◁ Festooned with pink baubles, the common staghorn coral awaits the right moment for its annual spawning. Each bauble is actually a bundle of about eight pink eggs, with the testes wrapped among them. Only some young polyps around the growing tip have not produced an egg-sperm bundle.

◁ ▽ In the days before the spawning night, the gonads (sex organs) of the polyps are fully developed and waiting for their cue to spawn. This staghorn coral has been broken open to reveal the long cream testes attached at their tops to the mesenteries. Behind them can be seen a number of bright pink, mature eggs arranged singly along other mesenteries.

▽ The egg-sperm bundle held within the open mouth of Goniastrea palauwensis is suddenly released, and it will float quickly to the surface. The exact moment of release is captured in the two photographs below.

Goniastrea palauwensis

Goniastrea palauwensis

Galaxea fascicularis

Galaxea fascicularis

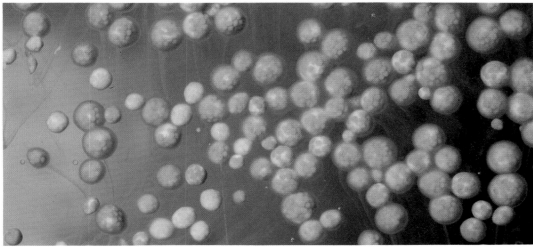

Coral eggs

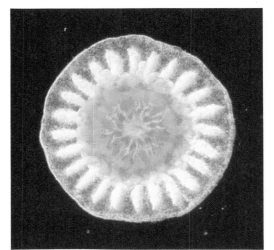

Coral planulae

△ *Before they spawn, the corals can be seen 'setting': all the polyps show a brightly coloured distension beneath the mouth disc. About fifteen minutes after this stage the egg-sperm bundles are pushed through the polyp mouths. Then the moment of release comes. Sometimes an entire colony will release within seconds, sometimes patches of the colony go in bursts. Frequently, all polyps release within about fifteen minutes.*

◁ *The egg-sperm bundles are large enough to be seen in the light of a torch directed at the water surface. At the peak of spawning the sea surface is dense with these brightly coloured little balls. Soon after reaching the surface, the bundle breaks up and the melee begins. Sperm streams out over the water, thousands from each bundle. Propelled by their long tails they travel, hopefully to collide with an egg of their own species, which they will fertilise. The fertilised egg will develop into a tiny swimming larva which will drift in the plankton for a few days before descending into the water column.*

◁ *A little polyp, about ten days old and two millimetres wide, already shows its affinity with the huge corals of the reef. Through its transparent tissues the beginnings of the white limestone skeleton can be seen. The fertilised coral larvae are called planulae, and mature corals are known to produce thousands of them at a time. When released by the parent, they swim upwards towards the sunlight. Then, before attaching themselves, they alter their behaviour and swim away from the light towards the sea bed. There they settle and build new colonies. Some settle near their parent colonies, but others are capable of floating for months in the surface waters. These are of great importance in distributing the species over a very wide area; the mortality rate during this early stage of the coral's life is extremely high.*

'*Acropora* polyps usually have four strings of eggs and two or four testes, each on a separate mesentery. All of these are gathered to make the egg-sperm bundle that will be released later.'

Montastrea

△ *In this coral, spawning is underway. The polyps at the bottom right are empty; in the centre the round egg-sperm bundles have been ejected and are rising; and at left they are still held in the polyp.*

▷ *Not all corals have male and female gonads together in the one polyp. In the mushroom corals, each individual is either male or female. This male mushroom coral is releasing a cloud of white sperm, which will have to find the eggs of a nearby female.*

▷▷ *Most egg-sperm bundles are buoyant, but this is not the case for* Goniastrea favulus, *where the sperm travel alone upwards as a white cloud. The eggs are sticky and negatively buoyant, falling to remain around the base of the colony, seemingly making it difficult for the two to get together.*

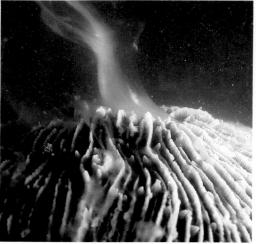

Mushroom coral, *Fungia*

Goniastrea favulus

Favites halicora

Mass spawning

'As the reef waters warm in the spring the coral sex cells develop rapidly. Eggs become coloured: pink, red or orange, sometimes even purple, blue or green.'

◁ *When there are too many eggs and testes for a single bundle, several bundles may be released. This is the case with Favites halicora, where eggs and testes can be seen in each of the little packages coming out of the polyp mouths. Many more await release, and appear as pink shading underneath the mouth discs.*

◁ ▽ *Many soft corals spawn at the same time as the hard corals. This unidentified species has released individual eggs, which are clinging to the surface of the green polyps.*

▽ *The separate mouths of the joined polyps of a brain coral still release their separate egg–sperm bundles. The tentacles of this brain coral have retracted because of artificial lighting.*

Soft coral

Brain coral, *Platygyra sinensis*

Staghorn coral, *Acropora florida*

Staghorn coral, *Acropora listeri*

△ *Closely related animals or plants usually reproduce at different times of the year and thus avoid the possibility of hybridization. However, many species of staghorn coral spawn on the same night of the year releasing egg-sperm bundles. The evolutionary pressures to do such a paradoxical thing must be very powerful.*

'Scientists are puzzled about how a coral sperm manages to find the right mate. Perhaps the answer lies in the chemical make-up of the eggs.'

Staghorn coral, *Acropora secale*

New life for old

The reef has seasons of change and constancy, and these can be seen in the reproductive patterns of corals and the settling patterns of their larvae. Other changes are less regular. Rough weather can bring big changes, causing the branches of tree-like corals to snap and large coral tables to tumble down the reef slope, destroying and taking with them an avalanche of other corals.

Such movement will cause the death of some corals that cannot withstand the effects of the change of position. For others, the movement is an opportunity for asexual reproduction by breaking into many parts. For many reef organisms, shifting coral means a piece of cleared space, and those who are in the right place at the right time then compete for its occupancy.

The nature and scale of possible changes are almost limitless. A population explosion of the crown-of-thorns starfish, *Acanthaster planci*, for example, may leave thousands of corals dead, and much clear space. One fast-growing coral plate may expand and block out the space in the light for the slower growing species below it. Perhaps such changes benefit corals, whose primary aim in life seems to be to find, maintain and if possible expand upon, a suitable place in which to live.

◁ *Ripe coral eggs are usually brightly coloured in shades of pink or red, but this species spawns bundles of brilliant blue eggs.*

◁ ▽ *This big plate of table coral was over a metre across and about ten years old when it snapped from its stalk and fell 12 metres from the reef top to a bed of staghorn coral on the sandy reef floor. It did not survive the fall, and its dead tissues sloughed away, leaving a clean limestone surface full of nooks and crannies — just the spot for tiny larvae and algae spores to settle. Little yearling corals, mostly about 15 months old, can be seen on its surface. The staghorn corals that broke its fall are now beginning to grow up around it.*

◁ *Twenty months after the first picture, the corals, now three years old, have grown large enough to make their presence obvious. Many have not survived, being eaten in their first, second or third year by grazing animals, being overgrown by other young corals or expanding organisms, or simply suffering the consequences of having settled in the wrong place. They now face another growing problem: competition for space from the surrounding staghorn corals that are thriving and winning back the space that was previously theirs.*

Favia favus

Table coral, *Acropora cytherea*

Table coral, *Acropora cytherea*

Whip coral, *Junceella fragilis*

△ *Some of the most novel methods of asexual reproduction are shown by Gorgonians and soft corals. This whip coral is usually found in clumps – a good clue for asexual reproduction. As the whips grow, small pieces are pinched off at their tops. This is done by degeneration of the tissues along a small portion of the whip, until only the central horny rod remains. This is broken by the slightest water movement, and the bud drops to the reef floor, where it cements itself before commencing growth into a new whip. Some buds land upside down, and have to change their direction of growth, leaving a record on the base of the whip of their asexual origin.*

'The most successful corals in seemingly inhospitable places are those which can produce new colonies by asexual means, cloning from one originally settled larva.'

Hard coral, *Acropora*

Soft coral, *Efflatounaria*

△ *Coral larvae require a hard surface on which to settle. Such sites abound on the solid reef, but on the sandy reef floor they are restricted to bits and pieces of dead coral and shells. Lots of staghorn and bottle-brush forms of the hard coral genus* Acropora *settle these areas. As the colonies grow, parts of them become buried in the sand and the polyps die. Those parts become weakened by the action of various boring animals, but the parts beyond them are still living. The final outcome is a mass of many colonies that may cover several square metres of reef floor.*

◁ *Soft corals very commonly employ asexual reproduction. This soft coral produces a long stolon like a strawberry runner, which grows out and away from the colony. Once this finds an agreeable piece of surface it stops extending, attaches itself, and proceeds to grow a new daughter colony. This process can be repeated many times and little groups of parent and offspring like this are a common sight on some areas of the reef.*

Asexual reproduction

Corals have another recourse, apart from spawning, to ensure the continued survival of their own types. Because they are modular organisms, with polyps replicated many times over, some corals break up in various ways so that one colony creates more colonies, without the complicated process of producing juveniles.

There are many beneficial consequences of such behaviour: more colonies mean more chances that the organism will survive; asexual reproduction can take place at any time of the year; and the offspring, sometimes known as 'daughter colonies', do not have to face the vicissitudes of planktonic life in a larval stage.

Other benefits are less obvious: in places that are too silty or too crowded for the settlement of tiny larvae, such problems can be avoided by producing offspring that are already adult.

The modes of asexual reproduction vary from relatively unsophisticated means, such as pieces snapping off in storms, to ingenious devices such as the colony pinching off small portions or sending out runners. One of the features of this kind of reproduction is that the offspring stay close to the parent colony, so that a group of similar colonies – a clone – results.

Feeding

Corals are carnivores and catch food from the surrounding waters by extending tentacles armed with stinging nematocyst cells. Microscopic floating animals – zooplankton – trigger the firing of these barbed darts, which paralyse and hold them. The tentacles then pass the morsel to the mouth of the polyp with a graceful bending motion. The prey is broken down in the polyp stomach and becomes part of the nutrition for the whole colony.

Black coral, *Cirrhipathes*

Hard coral, *Trachyphyllia geoffroyi*

Soft coral, *Sarcophyton*

Most hard corals feed in this way at night, while many other coral kin feed at any time, night or day. They take a variety of small animals: shrimps and their relatives; eggs and larval stages of many reef invertebrates; even, in the case of some large polyps, tiny reef fishes. Some corals also ensnare bacteria and zooplankton in nets of mucus, a slimy substance manufactured by the polyps. Organic materials dissolved in sea water passing through the polyps also supply some of the needs of the polyp tissues. When a soft coral feeds, this process can sometimes be seen in many polyps at once, with a half dozen plankton being caught and moved into the mouth. Some of the common soft corals of the family Xeniidae open and close their large polyps, which look like tiny grasping hands. However, as these animals rely almost totally on their symbiotic zooanthellae for nourishment and do not feed on plankton, the reason for this pulsating is still a mystery.

△ *This young soft coral feeds during the day with polyps expanded and tentacles unfolded to ensnare the minute zooplankton floating past in the water currents.*

◁ △ *The coiled spring of the black coral waits for planktonic organisms to drift into the clutches of its yellow polyps. Water turbulence around the coil may cause the plankton to linger momentarily, giving the coral a feeding advantage over its straighter relatives.*

◁ *Hard corals feed at night with tentacles expanded, displaying the little clumps of concentrated stinging cells that will immobilise prey.*

Association and conflict

The interaction between corals and other organisms is many and varied. Mobile reef animals seek shelter and food within and around the boundaries of a coral colony. However, since corals are modular organisms with many polyps in each colony, interference with parts of the colony does not represent the calamity it would to unitary organisms. Individual polyps, or even groups of polyps, can be eaten, damaged or nudged aside without destroying the rest of the colony. Few predators are large enough to eat entire colonies.

Corals have various ways of dealing with the intrusion of other colonial animals, including other corals, sometimes drawing up 'battle lines' with their neighbours, sometimes growing up or away in another direction.

For mutual benefit

In many cases the nutrition that corals obtain by feeding is sufficient for their existence. It is supplemented, however, through a remarkable association with their inhabiting zooxanthellae, which in effect creates super-corals from what would otherwise be insignificant, small animals. The relationship between the two is complex and not yet fully understood. Each seems to complement the nutritional needs of the other, and the zooxanthellae significantly enhance the coral's ability to build skeletons. The mutual benefits to coral and algae make this special association a symbiosis, and the reef-builder that results from the association is called a hermatype.

Zooxanthellae are algal cells of a species *Gymnodinium microadriaticum*, which is also able to exist independently in the sea water. In their free-living state these cells are moved by two long fine tails called flagellae, but those living in the coral have no flagellae. They live inside cells in the coral tissue, where they are able to take in carbon dioxide (a byproduct produced as the cell uses oxygen). This is used in photosynthesis: the process by which plants absorb the energy of sunlight and manufacture materials needed for growth and continued existence. Some of these materials are passed to the coral, and other products from the coral are also used by the algae.

Solar cells

Many of the habits of corals are explained by the presence of zooxanthellae. Since they are little solar cells, requiring exposure to sunlight for their operation, they only perform during the day and they can only function in shallow regions where sunlight penetrates. Their hosts, the reef-building corals, thus restrict themselves to shallow, well-lit waters – living coral reefs are therefore only a shallow-water phenomenon. Another consequence is seen in the shape of coral colonies. Many corals that form various shapes in shallow water are

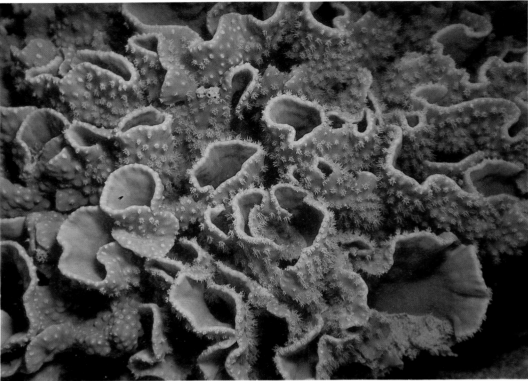

Hard coral, *Turbinaria mesenterina*

▽ *When the tissues of a reef-building coral are magnified, thousands of the little algal cells, zooxanthellae, can be seen. These are the non-motile or encysted stages of certain species of algae. These tiny plants obtain shelter from their life in the coral cells. In return they act as a solar powerhouse for the coral and endow it with the special ability to play a part in the construction of a coral reef. However, the proportion of a coral's nutritive requirements provided by zooxanthellae is not known.*

△ *The polyps of this hard coral are arranged on the upper surface of thin plates. It abounds on muddy inshore reefs where light cannot penetrate far through the murky water; a difference of about a metre in depth makes a striking difference to the amount of light energy reaching the coral surface. By its growth form this coral is able to position zooxanthellae to catch the sun's rays. Where there is an unlimited supply of sunlight, the plates are folded into extravagant patterns that place the polyps and their tissue connections in variously shaded positions.*

▷ *In deeper water, where available light is at a premium, colonies of this hard coral grow as spreading plates, with the polyps and tissues fully exposed to take every possible advantage of the waning sunlight. The difference in colony shapes is so striking that they appear to be two different species. However, a convoluted colony, transferred to deeper water, changes its style of growth in an attempt to flatten out into a plate. This is a slow process because the coral cannot alter skeleton that was existing before the move.*

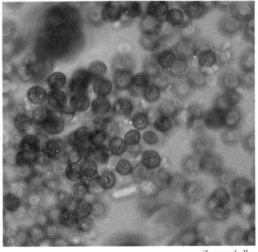

Zooxanthellae

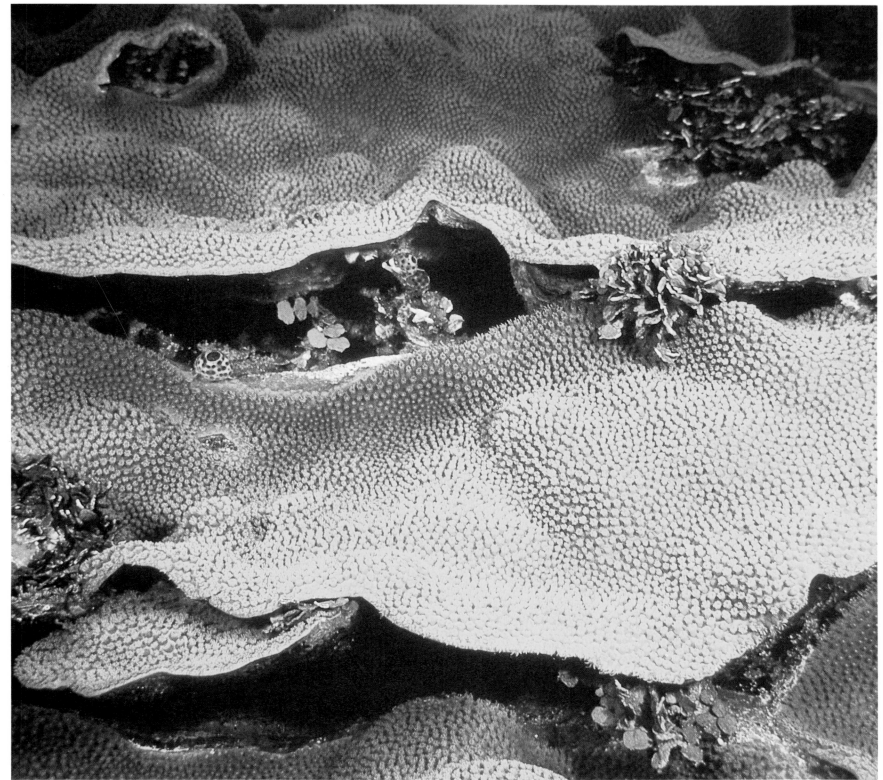

Hard coral, *Turbinaria mesenterina*

Hard coral, *Porites*

Button coral, *Heteropsammia cochlea*

flattened out when they occur in deeper water, demonstrating the importance of light-capturing in the life of a reef-building coral.

A coral resident

Heteropsammia cochlea is a little coral with a unique life style. It has only one or two polyps and lives unattached on the sandy inner-reef floor. Every specimen of this coral has a sipunculid or peanut worm, *Aspidosiphon corallicola*, inhabiting its skeleton. The foraging activities of the peanut worm keep the coral from becoming buried in the reef sediments and stabilise it in an upright position. The coral invariably occurs in association with the worm, which seems to be fundamental to its existence on the soft, unstable sea floor.

The peanut worm settles from a floating, planktonic existence to become a bottom dweller by inhabiting a tiny snail shell. As it grows it sheds smaller shells for larger ones. About this time the larva of *Heteropsammia cochlea* is metamorphosing into an adult coral by attaching itself to the shell inhabited by the worm. The peanut worm now has no need to seek further accommodation, which is often a problem for larger worms. Instead, it modifies the developing coral skeleton to maintain an entrance hole and a series of small holes around the coral's periphery. The entrance allows the worm to extend from the skeleton for foraging and for moving its coral house along. The small holes

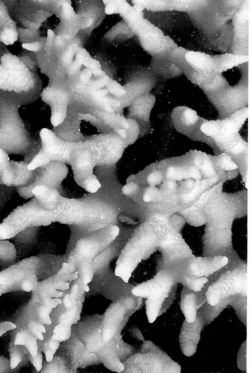

Needle coral, *Stylophora pistillata*

△ *This solitary little coral lives on the sandy inter-reef floor with a tenant peanut worm. The tenant's dimple-like 'windows' (for the passage of water currents) are along the side of the coral, which is digesting a yellow fish, seen through the swollen transparent mouth disc.*

△ ◁ *Corals can play host to a large number of tenants, without appearing to suffer from their presence. This mound of small-polyped hard coral is inhabited by tubes of the Christmas-tree worm, Spirobranchus giganteus, which occurs in many colours and will withdraw its feathery feeding appendages at the slightest disturbance.*

◁ *Coral skeletons are often modified to grow around small animals such as crabs, shrimps and barnacles. This needle coral forms elegant little shell-shaped cysts around its guests, the crabs Hapalocarienus marsupialis.*

'The hard corals have been aptly described as the architects of the reef. The limestone of their skeletons is in the form of needle-shaped crystals that fit together in fan-shaped tufts.'

are used for drawing in water for respiration and expelling it again.

This coral can occur in huge populations, and each coral is either male or female. After it settles it becomes dependent on the peanut worm; the worm, however, can exist without the coral.

Being eaten

Few animals kill a whole coral colony when they feed on it. Exceptions are the crown-of-thorns starfish and the buffalo fish, avid predators. The crown-of-thorns starfish can eventually kill even large coral plates as a single specimen sometimes returns to the same colony nightly until the entire plate is eaten; during population explosions, many starfish may feed on one colony. Other animals, particularly some small gastropod molluscs, feed on coral tissues and can damage large areas of them when feeding in big groups.

Crown-of-thorns starfish, *Acanthaster planci*

Buffalo fish, *Bolbometaphon muricatuin*

△ *Buffalo fish bite large chunks from corals, leaving characteristic wounds. Both tissue and skeleton are taken, but sometimes part of the colony survives the attack. The wounds are often colonised by algae that remain as patches on the surface of the coral.*

◁ △ *The crown-of-thorns starfish is a persistent coral predator. When present in large numbers, this species kills whole colonies by digesting the coral tissue and leaving a clean skeleton.*

◁ *When a coral encounters another coral or colonial organism as it grows, a number of alternative strategies are available to it. If it is a branching coral it may grow up and over or away from its neighbour. If it is an encrusting coral, such as the purple* Montipora *and grey* Hydnophora, *it may grow over its neighbours.*

Encrusting corals, *Montipora* and *Hydrophora*

'On the reef there are no hard and fast rules about which coral should appear where and what blendings of species may occur.'

▷ *Various mobile animals feed on and around corals without damaging the coral polyps. Nudibranchs, like this primitive sea slug,* Chelidonura inornata, *scavenge bacteria and detritus caught in the mucus which has been exuded by the coral.*

Hard coral, *Diploastrea heliopora*

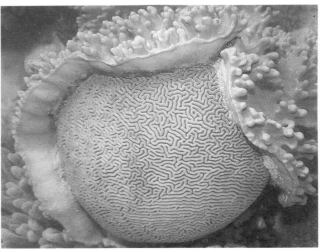

Hard coral, *Leptoria phrygia*; soft coral, *Sinularia densa*

△ *For many hard corals, confrontation with neighbours involves the formation of a no-man's-land by the action of long sweeping tentacles or extended stomach filaments, which kill and sometimes devour coral tissue. Many soft corals have the added advantage of toxic chemical defences. The outcome of such encounters depends on the relative skills of the contenders. This hard coral appears to be succumbing to the invasion of a soft coral.*

Visual dominants

Every coral reef has unique features, but some patterns are repeated in similar circumstances. There are plateaux – the reef flats – where the top of the reef is exposed to full sunlight, where temperatures may fluctuate greatly, and where the watery environment may come and go with the flow of the tide. Sometimes the reef encloses a lagoon – a protected pool with sandy bottom and scattered patches of coral. At the edge of this flat the waves break, especially on the 'weather side' where the reef faces the prevailing winds. From the reef top, the slope descends to the sea floor: sometimes gently, sometimes as a steep cliff face. Strong currents may run along this face, and deep channels may intercept it at regular intervals. The effects of wind and sea play a part in the sculpturing of the reef, thereby influencing the suitability of areas for the settlement of coral larvae or for the survival of different shapes

and types of colonies. Sometimes the effects of wind and sea even determine the form taken by modular colonies as they grow.

The corals inhabiting the reef change from place to place, influenced by many things: some obvious, some understood only after years of research, most still unknown and mysterious. Differences in life cycles, the ability to tolerate environmental conditions, the practicality of shapes for different physical situations and the plasticity employed in shaping a colony to suit the location all play a part. So, too, do influences beyond the control of the corals – the chance occurrence of a 'good' or 'bad' year for reproduction and settlement; the unexpected devastation of a cyclone, or the dilution of reef waters by flooding. Sweeping changes and small influences, working locally on a single portion of the reef, all play a part in making the completion of its pattern a game of chance as well as strategy.

Exposed coral head

Exposed corals

Ridge coral, *Acropora palifera*

△ *Any reef, no matter how rich and luxuriant its overall coral composition, has places where few corals grow. Other parts of the reef flat, where water flows freely, may support coral cover so rich that a reef walker might be well advised to avoid them. During some of the very low spring tides, these corals are exposed to the air for some hours, above and left. While they will usually be able to tolerate this, any added difficulty, such as a heavy rain squall or unusually hot or cold conditions, can cause massive local death to exposed corals.*

◁ *Reef fronts exposed to the influences of prevailing winds and full ocean swells support a coral community which resists these forces with sturdy, stunted growths. This ridge of staghorn coral has blunt blades aligned perpendicularly to the reef edge, despite the fact that it can occur with long branches on more sheltered parts of a reef.*

Plate coral, *Montipora foliosa*

Coral microatoll, *Porites*

△ The combination of hard corals and large fields of algae is a common sight on the fringing reefs around islands near the tropical coast. The scene in these coral–algal fields is constantly changing with the seasons, as the algae follow an annual cycle of settlement, growth, reproduction, and breakdown of the old colonies. This plate coral is shadowed by a field of Sargassum *towers.*

▷ △ Corals growing on the reef flat encounter a barrier – the water surface at mid-tide level – above which coral tissue simply cannot survive. The presence of this barrier has led to a fascinating form of coral growth in which the colony continues to expand around its radius, but is dead on top. As the colony gets older, the dead patch may become hollowed out, and other corals may settle in the shallow lagoon so formed. These formations resemble miniature coral atolls and they are referred to as 'microatolls'. Many coral species can grow this way and on some parts of a reef flat there are hundreds of microatolls to be found.

▷ This mound-like outline is achieved by branching colonies. Some parts of reefs, whether due to accidents of history or to special characteristics of the environment, support a coral assemblage that is predominantly marked by one shape. As far as the eye can see, this patch of sandy reef lagoon is dominated by colonies of a single species of Porites *coral.*

Coral mounds, *Porites cylindrica*

Branching coral, *Porites cylindrica*

Suiting the location

'Some parts of reefs, whether due to accidents of history or special environmental characteristics, support a coral assemblage where one shape of coral colony predominates markedly.'

Reef slope, Myrmidon Reef

△ *Some corals have great plasticity of form, being able to vary the colony shape from mounds to sheets or from branches to plates. Something has caused considerable death within this acid-yellow colony of branching coral, exposing the white skeleton of the dead portions. The remaining live patches of the colony have spread out as plates around their bases.*

◁ *Hard and soft corals living on the reef slope must cling to the reef surface and at the same time must spread out their surfaces to catch the light. This steep slope supports a large variety of species.*

The protean staghorns

Acropora, the staghorn coral, has more species, grows faster, and occupies more reef than any other coral. The most beautiful reef scenes are set against a backdrop of a luxuriant covering of *Acropora*.

Its shapes range far wider than the general name implies: table, plate, bottle-brush and shrub are among them. Some individual species cover the whole range, varying their colony shapes to suit their particular location. Others are rigidly confined to a single shape. *Acropora* has been described as 'the protean coral genus' – an allusion to Proteus, the god fabled for his habit of changing his form to confuse and elude.

Acropora species seem to thrive in areas with plenty of water movement and sunshine. It is quick to colonise places where corals have been damaged, and many of its species regenerate from broken fragments. It appears to be a very hardy coral, but paradoxically it is very difficult to keep most species alive for more than a few days in aquaria.☐

▷ *Staghorn coral growing in two of its starkly contrasting forms: below,* Acropora nobilis, *in the form that gives the coral its common name; above, a magnificent table of* A. cytherea. *The tables begin as small compact bushes, the branches growing first upwards to form the stem, and later outwards and upwards so that an intermediate 'vase' shape is formed. The top of the table bears little branchlets on which the polyps are densely packed.*

▷ *Tables or plates of staghorn coral thrive and grow in abundance on the very shoulder of a reef. Paradoxically, as they grow, their vulnerability increases. Strong waves whipped up by high winds can snap them from their · stalks, and they go crashing to the reef floor below, sometimes taking an avalanche of other corals with them. The reef shows the scars of such events in patchy patterns of distribution of large and small plates.*

'A branch of *Acropora* coral has a large, cylindrical polyp as its axis, and other polyps are budded from around the tip of this as it grows.'

Staghorn coral, *Acropora nobilis, A. cytherea*

Staghorn coral, *Acropora*

Staghorn coral, *Acropora listeri*

◁ *One colony or many? This huge old colony shows the versatility of Acropora growth. Portions of the colony resembling sturdy hands die off around their bases, so the colony effectively has many separated parts. This growth form is seen in places with strong currents, such as channels between outer reefs, where many species of staghorn coral may take the same shape.*

◁ ▽ *This coral has close relatives in the Montipora genus, which mainly occurs as thin plates. Rarely is a reef seen which does not include one or other of these genera.*

▽ *Staghorn coral is a familiar sight to reef walkers who venture to the reef's edge, where the genus reigns supreme. Low tables, bushes and shrubs of staghorn thrive in the well-aerated waters provided by the breaking of waves on the reef.*

Bottlebrush coral, *Acropora echinata*

Staghorn coral, *Acropora*

Diverse and beautiful

'One of the most remarkable features of *Acropora* corals is the fact that so many species occur together. In the animal world "close relatives" generally spells competition for food resources.'

▷ *Few divers are treated to the sight of low, dense* Acropora *cover, which is characteristic of high current banks on outer reefs.*

▽ *The intricate branching patterns of staghorn corals make them excellent shelters for tiny fishes, which feed in and around the colonies, retreating into the branches when danger approaches. Towards dusk, staghorn patches become clouded by these fishes as they come out to feed in their thousands.*

Staghorn coral, *Acropora yongei*

Staghorn coral, *Acropora monticulosa, A. listeri* and *A. gemmifera*

Staghorn coral, *Acropora horrida* and *A. lovelli*

Christmas coral, *Acropora elseyi*

Staghorn coral, *Acropora grandis*

Staghorn coral, *Acropora*

△ Some of the prettiest reef scenes are those completely dominated by staghorn corals. Their beauty and variety make these 'coral garden' sites favourites with divers.

◁ △ It is an axiom of animal ecology that two species with exactly the same resource requirements cannot co-exist; however, the requirements of many Acropora appear to be very similar, and most species reproduce at the same time. The co-existence of so many species is a fascinating puzzle.

◁ △ Bottlebrush Acropora abound in the more protected waters of the reef, where they may occupy huge tracts of sandy reef floor. This large colony of Christmas coral shows the typical elegant form that makes it a favourite of the coral curio trade.

◁ Some reef sites support dense groupings of colonies of many Acropora species, but in other places single majestic colonies grow in splendid isolation.

Giant clams

Part three: life above and among corals

Strange are the stories told about the animals and plants that live in the different kinds of habitats on the Great Barrier Reef and its wild islands, seemingly timeless, yet constantly changing. Strange indeed – and difficult to believe – but very real. Many hundreds of new species are yet to be described, and for scientists or the casual observer there is still much to learn.

A lot of the activity in the water above the reef is invisible, except to the sharp-eyed observer. One small floating animal builds a large, gossamer fishing net to trap fine plankton, and drifts with its net in the tropical waters. Boring sponges chemically digest the limestone skeleton of corals during the search for living space, using a mechanism resembling an ice-cream scoop. As the sponges bore they weaken the coral skeleton, which then crumbles during storms.

Sponges and ascidians constantly filter vast quantities of water through their tissues. A small ascidian, only 30 millimetres long, can filter water at the rate of approximately one litre an hour.

The lowly worm is abundant on the reef. Who would guess that one coral head, 450 millimetres across, would contain over 1200 individual small burrowing worms of over 100 different species. The

peanut worm, so-called because of its shape, lives in the skeleton of a little coral with only one or two polyps, and carries it around on its foraging expeditions. This keeps the coral from becoming buried in reef sediments and keeps it upright. Many creatures on the reef live in similarly supportive relationships.

Down in the coral city are thousands of crustaceans – the insects of the sea. One strange little crustacean finds a salp with a firm, gelatinous home, about 10 to 20 millimetres long, and lives on the salp until it has eaten it away; the crustacean is left with a useful, barrel-shaped house, open at each end.

In the David and Goliath category is a very small shrimp that will attack the crown-of-thorns starfish, a hundred times its size, tearing into one after the other of its soft tube feet and often forcing the giant to leave the coral it was about to consume.

On land, too, much is not as it seems. The coral cays, with their lovely *Pisonia* trees and silver *Argusia* shrubs, are not inhabited by a stable set of animals and plants. Many of the smaller species are changing constantly; a different set of insects and spiders may be present, or a new herb may cover the sparse soil, from year to year. A delicate balance exists between a constant stream of immigrants and a continuous series of extinctions, as animals and plants fail to build stable populations on a small and often harsh terrain. Perennial visitors are the turtles; as many as 10 000 may leave the sea to lay eggs at the same time on an island.

So little is known about the animals and plants of the reef as yet; the life histories of only a few score of the tens of thousands of species have been studied. But with each detailed exploration, new and strange living patterns are found. □

◁ *Giant clams, corals and tropical fishes are the trademark of the coral reef. The jumbled profusion of life which stuns the visitor to the reef is a fragile ecosystem dependent on clear, clean water for its continued existence. Unless the tropical sun can penetrate to the microscopic plants living in the tissues of the corals and giant clams, they are unable to grow and provide the places for other reef animals to live and hide.*

▷ *A whale disturbs the surface of the calm clear waters of the reef as it rises to breathe. Although some whales are awesome divers and can reach depths of hundreds of metres, they are mammals and must breathe air. Marine reptiles – sea snakes and turtles – must also surface for air, unlike most animals living in and around the corals.*

Pilot whale

Symbiosis: secret success of the reef

Survival in the desert

The Great Barrier Reef is an oasis in a watery desert – a desert, because almost nothing grows in the low-nutrient waters of most tropical seas. Phosphate, nitrogen, iron and other essential nutrients are barely detectable in the clear, sunlit waters; clear, because so little is growing. A vibrant, living coral reef in such clear water is a miracle of evolution and nature's biological ingenuity.

Coral chemical factory

Collaboration is the secret of success and progress in the reef. The biologist's term 'symbiosis' denotes a special kind of collaboration. To survive in a sea with no nitrogen or phosphate nutrients would be impossible for algae. To survive without a supply of energy-rich food would be impossible for animal life. The corals solved the problem millions of years ago: their animal cells engulfed microscopic algae and confined them; one algal cell in each animal cell in the inner of the coral's two cell layers. The alga is in reality a solar cell that can convert the sun's light energy into chemical energy. This is done through photosynthesis, by which a plant produces food and oxygen. With plenty of light and plenty of carbon dioxide in the water, algae can produce limitless food, provided they have the necessary nitrogen and phosphate to maintain their chemical factory. Inside the animal cell, this is no problem. The animals produce nitrogen in the form of ammonia, which is absorbed by the alga. Instead of trying to survive in the sea, the symbiotic algae of the coral thrive within it. They have no shortage of nutrients, unlike their relatives struggling in the seas outside.

The alga gives up to 80 per cent of the products of its photosynthesis to its host. Ordinary algae cannot do that, nor can coral algae once they are removed from the coral. But when the algae are exposed to the corals' digestive enzymes, the algae become leaky. Glycerol (a sugar-like compound) and nutritious amino acids leak from the alga and are used by the animal. Together, the coral and alga thrive. With much less need for food from the outside, the coral can dominate the reef where independent, less efficient creatures could not.

Coral symbiosis is the major one of many such biological systems operating on the reef – as efficient as the best industrial chemical factory.

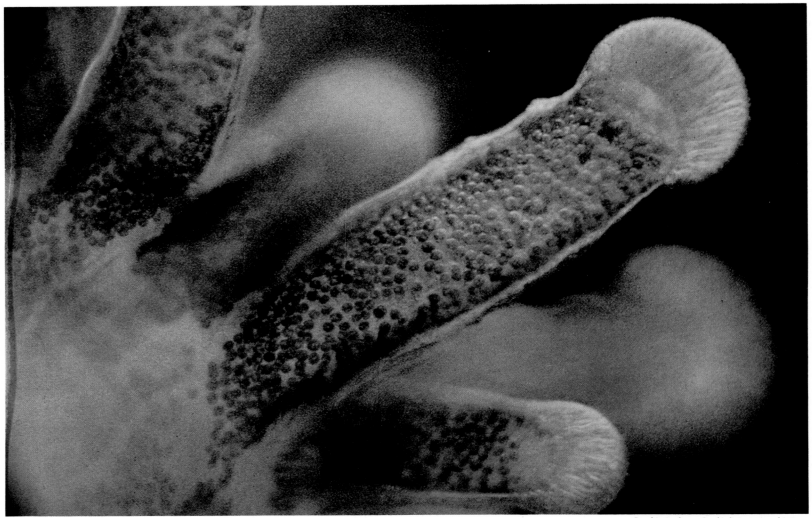

Symbiotic algae, *Symbiodinium microadriaticum*

Adapting to blue light

Algae have also adapted to the blue light that penetrates farthest into the sea. The symbiotic algae of corals appear to be the same species, *Symbiodinium microadriaticum*, although there are probably many subspecies. They are coloured by the golden brown algal pigments that are capable of absorbing blue light. Most undersea photographs reveal this blueness. The algae have adapted to depth and shading from overhanging rock or other corals by increasing the amount of chlorophyll in their chloroplasts. Like sun plants (such as corn and cactus) and shade plants (such as ferns and camellias) algae's apparatus for photosynthesis is well adapted to their light environment.

Almost half of the earth's sedimentary rocks are produced from the calcareous skeletons of surface-living single-celled foraminifera called forams, that settle on the sea floor. Beaches near the Great Barrier Reef are often made of such skeletons. Most of the foraminifera of the upper light zone of the sea contain the same symbiotic algae – the secret of their success.

Living with clams and sponges

Not all successful symbiosis involves algae living within the host animal's cells. The giant clams, *Tridacna*, harbour the same dinoflagellate (red-tide) algae in their often colourful mantles. The mantles extend and contract as light intensity changes, depending upon their need to free their blood of waste ammonia. Unlike the corals, giant clams can harvest their algae as they multiply in the mantle: the clam's faeces contain both digested and still-living zooxanthellae – the symbiotic golden brown algae, so named because they are yellowish brown (xanthos) and living in the animal (zoos). The suffix 'ellae' is typical of many algal names.

◁ *In each cell of the coral's inner layer lives a single captive dinoflagellate alga called a zooxanthella. Instead of starving in the nutrient-poor tropical ocean, the zooxanthella thrives on the waste products of the host cell. Its chlorophyll collects solar energy with which the alga builds sugars, amino acids and fats to repay its hosts for its productive environment. This group, known as red-tide when they are growing rapidly at sea, includes the symbiotic zooxanthellae of clams, corals and anemones. These dinoflagellate algae seem to have developed the capability for being selected, invading and thriving within their many hosts.*

Foram, *Marginapora vertebralis*

'Deep sea algae get the blues. Blue light penetrates farthest into the sea, and deep-living algae are well-adapted to exploiting this light environment. Depth and shading from overhanging rocks are accommodated by an increase in the algae's chlorophyll content.'

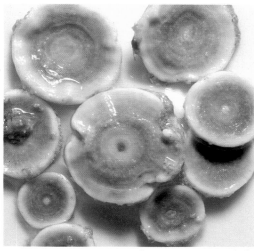

Foram, *Marginapora vertebralis*

◁ *Forams, left, above and top, are a large class of single-celled animals with calcareous skeletons. This species, which measures five to twelve millimetres in diameter, like most others in tropical waters carries symbiotic algae that use its waste products and the sun's energy to produce sugars and amino acids for its own food requirements. Forams can use their tiny pseudopodia to walk at surprising rates. Their skeletal remains make up many island beaches near the reef, and, indeed, half of the calcareous sedimentary rocks of the earth were formed at the sea bottom from countless skeletons of microscopic forams that lived in the upper light zone of the sea, but whose skeletons ultimately settled to the bottom.*

Foram, *Marginapora vertebralis*

Many sponges of the reef also harbour symbiotic algae and bacteria. The pink algae of the sponges differ from the dinoflagellates of corals and clams, and they, too, have adapted to the blue light. Sponges' algae are the blue-green *Cyanophyta* which possess a red-coloured protein that can absorb energy from the sun and pass it to the chlorophylls of the alga for photosynthesis. The exchange of light energy, nutrients and metabolic products serves the host sponge in its nutrient-impoverished environment.

Transferring goods and services
The inner layer of the two cell layers of a coral contains one algal cell in each animal cell. Just how the coral cell selects and engulfs its alga remains a mystery. Under stress, the coral will spit out the alga. The rapidly growing tips of the staghorn and other corals are often white and devoid of algae. One would think that this part of the coral would most need the energy collected by the algae, but nature has decided otherwise.

Algae absorb ammonia. As the waste ammonia from the animal's protein metabolism increases, the alga absorbs it and, with its copious light energy, reuses it for making amino acids, the building stones for the animal's proteins. The simplest amino acid for the alga to assemble is the compound alanine. The host can use alanine for new proteins, or use it for energy to drive the animal's muscles and pumping system.

Sea water contains an abundance of bicarbonate, a form of carbon dioxide. The algae use bicarbonate and light energy to produce carbohydrates. Glycerol is one of these carbohydrates, a simple sugar-like compound, easily produced from the alga's own sugars. When glycerol leaks from the algal cell, the animal host can use it to provide energy for work and growth. Thus, the coral has a daily supply of energy to drive its pulsating polyps in their quest for more nitrogen and phosphorous compounds from small zooplankton they might capture. The clams need extra energy for pumping the torrents of water that bathe their gills and plankton-collecting cilia.

The secret of coral productivity
The discovery that symbiotic algae leak their products of photosynthesis when living inside their hosts has revealed the secret of coral productivity,

'Coral symbiosis is one of the most efficient biological systems operating on the reef – its efficiency rivals that of the best chemical factory.'

Hard corals, *Stylophora pistillata*, *Symphyllia radians* and *Acropora lutkeni*

and has made it clear that symbiosis was the key to the reef's vitality. Without the alga, excess ammonia would suffocate the host. Without the host, the alga would starve; it could barely survive alone on the reef.

A third medium of exchange between host and zooxanthella is acetate, the neutralised form of acetic acid or vinegar. Acetate is produced by both the coral animal and the clam, as it is a nearly final oxidation product of most foods. Algae absorb the acetate and use their energy to reassemble it in long energy-rich chains of fatty acids that stabilise their chloroplasts. The fatty acids are transferred to the outer membrane of the alga, the animal's enzymes take them into its own cells, and it is formed into a product similar to cetyl palmitate, the most common wax of corals. When a small brain coral is immersed in solvent to extract its fats and oils and the solvent is then evaporated, the residue is a mass

△ *The brownish colour of most corals is that of their symbiotic golden brown algae. Apart from their heavy calcium carbonate skeleton, the corals are actually half plant and half animal. Sometimes superficial pigments may conceal the brown colour, resulting from a combination of the chartreuse and red-orange pigments that absorb the blue light penetrating waters of the reef. The deeper the sea and the more blue the light, the darker and browner the corals. The algae, thriving within their colourless coral animal host cells, can contribute over half of the products of their photosynthesis to their host.*

Giant clam, *Tridacna maxima*

of solid cetyl palmitate, which is also an important component of sperm whale oil. If a dried coral had no calcareous skeleton, it could burn just as easily as a candle!

The great energy of the wax of corals at first perplexed biologists because, of all animals in the sea, the coral is least in need of a store of energy. It receives energy from the sun every day. But it is the coral's larvae that will need the wax. The small larva is released, loaded with fuel, for its possibly exhausting search for a suitable site for a new colony. Only then does it accumulate more zooxanthellae and begin to function as an effective symbiotic system.

In the sea, wax wards off starvation. It has the energy of ordinary fats, but it can only be digested one tenth as fast. Animals who live under a threat of starvation, such as the zooplankton and deep sea fish, usually maintain a store of wax in addition to

their usual and readily available energy supplies like fats, protein, and carbohydrates. Wax is a major energy source for animals of the sea.

Small reef fishes often get some of their food in the form of wax from the corals they live with. Corals exude mucus in their quest for small zooplankton and bacteria. This mucus is collected by fishes as they nip at the coral surfaces. The mucus, a protein holding a great deal of water, also contains fats and wax. These lipids are exuded with the mucus, much like a 'primordial milk'.

Nature is replete with symbiotic systems. Human cells interact with each other in co-operative fashion. Trees could hardly survive were it not for their fungal symbionts which collect nutrients for their roots. From human societies to nature's ecosystems, collaboration enhances efficiency for survival, and the creatures of the reef live by this essential rule of life.☐

△ *The blue, green, purple and yellow colours that adorn the extended mantles of the giant clams of this species create a pansy patch effect. The brilliant colours are produced by light diffraction by submicroscopic layers of crystalline non-coloured pigments. Nature's purpose for these colours is perplexing. They conceal the animals' three to ten millimetre-thick layer of photosynthetic symbiotic zooxanthellae, which use the energy of sunlight to produce food and consume waste ammonia for their animal hosts.*

Sponges: great survivors

The fossil record of some 650 million years ago shows sponges as probably the first multicelled animals. They still play an important role in the complex structural processes which form the solid structures we call coral reefs.

As the sponges bore into corals they weaken the skeletons, which eventually crumble during storms. The shattered skeletons are further broken down to rubble and eventually into coral sand. Through the long process of geological time these fine and coarse sediments are cemented together to form the reef rock which is the real base of the coral reefs. Sponges also clean the water by filtering out most of the tiny food particles, removing as much as 99 per cent. of all bacteria. □

Yellow burrowing sponge

△ *Some sponges rely totally on chimneys for feeding while the bulk of the body is buried deep in the coral rock. Fine pores and canals at the base of the chimney convey water down to the sponge and the outcurrent water passes out through the top of the chimney.*

▷ *Some sponges use chimney-like structures to increase the flow of water through the canals. The canals that expel the water are raised up into the currents and act like a chimney to draw water in through many small pores, lower down the body. Among the many large erect chimneys of this sponge, which grows in back reef areas, nestles a similarly coloured feather star.*

Yellow-red vasiform sponge

'Sponges are the most efficient vacuum cleaners of the sea.'

◁ *The erect tubes of this sponge are not only useful as chimneys but allow it to feed above the fine sediments that would otherwise block its feeding canals when it is half buried in fine sand.*

▽ *The largest proportion of sponge species have a mixture of fibres and spicules in their skeletons. The fibres of this thick yellow fan are reinforced with spicules embedded inside. Other spicules support the canals and protrude through the outer skin.*

Tubular sponge, *Clathria*

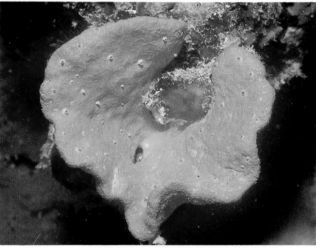

Thick yellow fan sponge, *Phakellia aruensis*

◁ *Most people know sponges by the fibrous skeletons that are the remains of only a small proportion of sponges after the cellular tissue has been removed. Sponges have a number of different skeleton types. The calcareous sponge has a skeleton consisting of millions of three-pointed and four-pointed stars (spicules) that are similar in composition to the calcium carbonate found in coral skeletons. These spicules, with the collagen fibres and cells that hold them together, support the sponge's canals and filter-feeding chambers.*

Calcareous sponge, *Pericharax heteroraphis*

Feather star, *Himerometra robustipinna*

Echinoderms: a zoological puzzle

Separate but similar

Five different kinds of closely related strange animals are, after fishes and corals, the most conspicuous creatures on the Great Barrier Reef ...

Bright, cobalt blue sea stars with five long, radiating arms lie draped over rubble in very shallow water. Under a nearby algae-covered piece of debris, a mass of thin, coiling arms resolves itself into an animal with a small, rounded body and five long, spiny arms – a brittle star – which proceeds to row jerkily away under the rubble.

In a deeper pool, dark green, sausage-shaped sea cucumbers lie quite still on the bottom. Others are black, with a light sprinkling of sand grains over their surface. The edge of the pool bristles with long black spines, waving menacingly; bright spots of red, iridescent blue and white reveal several sea urchins clustered there, each with a spherical body bearing numerous radiating spines.

Further out, attached to the top of a coral colony right on the reef's edge, the delicate arms of clusters of flower-like feather stars flutter in the gentle swell.

All five creatures – sea star, brittle star, sea cucumber, sea urchin and feather star – are echinoderms, and they respectively represent the five classes into which the phylum Echinodermata is usually divided: Asteroidea, Ophiuroidea, Holothurioidea, Echinoidea and Crinoidea.

Worldwide, these five classes include around 6000 species, 350 of which have so far been discovered living along the coast of Queensland and on the Great Barrier Reef itself.

Echinoderms are an ancient group of animals; their fossil ancestors are recognisable in rocks over 500 million years old, and today's living representatives are a mere remnant of the numbers known to have existed during their long history. Exclusively marine and almost all bottom-dwelling, they occur from between the tides to the deepest parts of the ocean. They are found both on hard, rocky substrates and in soft sediment; and while almost all are capable of some movement, many are sedentary.

Perhaps the most notorious echinoderm is the crown-of-thorns starfish. When their numbers build to thousands on a reef, the immediate result can be catastrophic, with up to 90 per cent of the coral being killed in some areas.□

◁ *More like some exotic crimson plant growing from the surface of the reef, it is hard to think of this as an animal at all, let alone an echinoderm. However, this beautiful animal with its many feather-like arms waving in the current is a common species of feather star, often forming clusters in the top few metres of water near the reef crest or festooning prominences on the sides of coral bommies.*

▷ *This beautiful urchin, while quite rare on the reef, is one of the most easily recognised. It has ten broad, naked areas on its body, and finely banded spines of equal length. Not growing large – adults are only 40 millimetres across – it is usually found under rubble. It grazes by night on hard surface areas.*

▷▷ *Most reef sea cucumbers feed on the soft sandy sediments of the lagoon floor. This animal, however, clambers over the hard substrate of the reef itself, unworried by sharp corals and the stinging cells lining their tentacles. Fully exposed by day but well camouflaged by its speckled brown colours, this species is a frequent sight on the reef slopes or sides of bommies.*

▷ *A common inhabitant of the shallow waters of the lagoonal patch reefs, the blue sea star is one of relatively few asteroids exposed by day. Perhaps its bright colour warns potential predators of the toxic substances within, thus making a nocturnal existence unnecessary.*

▷▷ *Much more active than the sea star, the brittle star crawls quickly using a rowing motion with its arms rather than its tube feet, which are used more for feeding. This species belongs to a group of predatory brittle stars that capture their prey by looping a lightning-fast arm coil around it then transferring it to the mouth.*

Sea urchin, *Mespilia globulus*

Sea cucumber, *Bohadschia graeffei*

Blue sea star, *Linckia laevigata*; brown sea star, *Nardoa novaecaledoniae*

Brittle star, *Ophiarachnella gorgonia*

▷ *Some feather stars, disliking strong currents, seek out quiet waters but they still require slight currents to bring their food.* Comanthina nobilis *lives in areas of medium strength current – it has no cirri but uses several of its arms with their spiny pinnules to anchor it to the reef.*

▽ *At first glance, the shape of a feather star shows little obvious similarity to its relatives the sea stars and brittle stars. Their orientation is different – both mouth and anus are located on the upper side of their small rounded body, which is set in a cup of interlocking calcareous plates.*

Feather star, *Comanthina nobilis*

Feather star, *Comanthus bennetti*

▷ *Crinoids can be very numerous in the areas of a reef where good currents flow. Such locations as along the ridges of a spur and groove system on the front slope, down the vertical walls of a deep channel between two reefs or on the sides of a back reef bombie may be dominated by hundreds of large feather stars, their bewildering array of patterns providing a riot of colour. Often prominently located, like these three feather stars, they are the most conspicuous echinoderms of the reef, rivalled only by the large sea cucumbers of the lagoon.*

Feather stars, *Comanthus bennetti*

Feather star, *Himerometra bartschi*

Suspension feeders

'Feather stars may have anything from five to over 200 arms, all of which radiate from five regions near the base; these arms are held in the current, trapping plankton.'

Feather star, *Comanthina nobilis*

△ Once a favoured position has been found by climbing or swimming, many feather stars that stay exposed by day will remain there permanently. Often their grasping cirri become overgrown with algae and other encrusting organisms. A tightly held sea whip or Gorgonian may die around the area grasped by the feather star. The immobility of feather stars has encouraged the mistaken concept that they are not animals but plants.

◁ Large feather stars with many arms adopt a hemispherical feeding posture. They are usually the species that grasp the substrate with their arms rather than using cirri. This brilliant yellow feather star has formed just such a bushy, multi-layered filtering device. It is also useful if the current direction is highly variable.

Yellow-faced angelfish, *Pomacanthus xanthometopon*

Fishes: brilliant, abundant and diverse

A confusion of species

There are more species of fishes on a coral reef than in any other place in the sea, and there is no land habitat, even a rainforest, that has a greater variety of vertebrates (amphibians, reptiles, birds, fishes and mammals). As the reef fishes glide over and about their coral caves and turreted coral castles they are closer to the birds of the air than any other animal, but they far surpass even the most exotic tropical birds in number, variety of colour, shape, and behaviour patterns. A small coral reef of less than a hectare may contain about 200 species. The whole Great Barrier Reef may have a remarkable 2000.

Every conceivable form of body shape and way of life have been adopted by this adaptable group of animals. The scientist has no satisfactory explanation for the questions of why so many species evolved and how they co-exist. The first question will always be speculative. The second can be observed, studied and tested, and yet remains a puzzle.

Many fishes have evolved with the corals, other invertebrates and their fellow fish species on the reefs to form an extremely integrated system. Close links between species show that evolution of one species is paralleled by the evolution of the other, an example of which is a relationship between a burrow-making shrimp and its 'look out' goby that depend on each other for survival. While there are many fishes that are obviously reef fishes, others found on the coral reef may also be found near the shore in rocky areas, or outside the coral reef zone. A precise definition of a 'coral reef fish' is difficult.

Sizing up the species

The smallest species on the reef are the tiny gobies, some of them so small that they sit, almost invisible, on the stalk of a sea whip, their two ventral fins fused to make a delicate sucker that grips the thin

◁ ◁ *Masks are popular among angelfish, and the yellow-faced angel has an elaborate one, with golden eye bar and blue mesh on its cheeks.*

▽ *The blue tuskfish is one of the larger wrasses, growing to one metre in length and with powerful crushing teeth. Adults will lift rocks aside with their mouths to get at crabs beneath them. This one is being groomed by a small wrasse, and is having its head picked clean of parasites.*

Blue tuskfish, *Choerodon schoenleinii*; wrasse, *Labroides dimidiatus*

◁ *A gracefully shaped shrub coral, Acropora, stands above the rest of the living reef in shallow water, its different sections inhabited by different species of fishes. Well above the coral a school of fusiliers feeds on plankton floating in the water. Below them, also feeding on plankton, are various damsels, but they remain close to the corals, relying on them for shelter. Other species will feed on the algae growing on the dead faces of the coral, and still further species will feed on small animals living on the sea bed. Fishes are found in many places on a coral reef. One fish species may be found only in deep caverns, another only in the lagoon, and another only in deeper water. There is still little understanding of how this great species mix is retained without some species out-competing others and driving them to extinction. But it is known that there are very subtle differences in the foods that are eaten, and in the choices of places to live.*

Fusiliers, *Caesio*; damsels, *Pomacentridae*

'A tiny goby weighing less than a gram has the same basic structure and body organs as the tiger shark, a million times its weight.'

▷ *Many of the smaller fishes on the reef have very delicate colours and lovely patterns. Cardinal fish, also unfortunately called gobbleguts, shun the bright light of the day, and school in the shelter of caverns, or under overhangs. Some, however, swim in the brighter light of the staghorn thickets. They tend to have delicate colours and patterns of red, silver and gold.*

Mandarin fish, *Synchiropus picturatus*

Δ *The mandarin fish is a little 100-millimetre species of the dragonet, Callionymidae, family and is found in shallow water. Little is known about this beautiful fish.*

▷ *The size of the coral polyps shows that this tiny goby is only about 20 millimetres long. Gobies are the smallest living animals with backbones.*

▷▷ *Trevallies or jack mackerels work along the reef edges for food, taking any unwary fishes, such as a plump fusilier that does not race away fast enough. Over 40 species are known in the Pacific Ocean, most of which are found on the reef. They are good angling fishes, usually taken with lures or fish bait, and many make good eating. The large turrum, growing to over 20 kilograms, is a member of this family.*

Cardinal fish, *Apogonidae*

Goby, *Tenacigobius*

Trevallies, *Carangidae*

◁ *There are giants among the bony fishes of the reef as well as the sharks and rays. The potato cod is not very common, except in a few places on the reef. Divers often find that the big cods are curious, even friendly. But they should be treated with caution.*

◁ ▽ *Manta rays are common in reef waters, and they are often seen leaping and falling back on the water surface with a resounding splash. This is said to be to remove parasites, but perhaps it is a display of territorial rights. A giant manta is harmless but it is an awesome sight underwater: two tonnes of large animal swimming by with strong and steady sweeps of its enormous wings.*

Potato cod, *Epinephelus tukula*

Manta ray, *Manta alfredi*

Tiger shark, *Galeocerdo cuvieri*

Whale shark, *Rhincodon typus*

stalk. Some are only ten millimetres long, and are probably the smallest animals with backbones that exist on earth. They weigh less than a gram, yet have the same basic structure and body organs – heart and blood system, kidney tissue, gonads, liver, brain, eyes, gills – that their huge relatives on the reefs do. One of the largest of these, the tiger shark, may grow to over 1000 kilograms, and therefore be a million times the size of its fellow reef dweller. There are fishes of every size between, and on any reef the majority of fishes are small. Damselfish weighing a few grams are common in swarms above the coral and there are many species of fishes under half a kilogram – small wrasses, goatfish, butterfly fish, a number of small rock cod species and fusiliers. Fishes of about one to two kilograms are fewer but include parrotfish, sweetlips and wrasses, as well as many of the medium-sized fish predators, such as many rock cods, hussars and

trevallies. Above this size, reaching 30 kilograms and more, are the large predators that roam the reef edges – Queensland mackerel, tuna, large trevallies like the turrum, and large barracuda. The final group are the giant sharks and rays, the marlins and their relatives, and the large rock cods.

The numbers of species and individuals go down rapidly as the size of the fish increases. There are thousands of small fishes on the reef, hundreds of medium-sized ones, tens of large ones, and the giants are very rare. In general the grazers are small and medium sized; the plankton feeders and those who feed on minute crustaceans are tiny; those feeding on most molluscs, crabs and shrimps are medium sized, and fish predators range from medium to enormous in size, depending on the size of their prey fishes. There are exceptions, however, such as the huge plankton-eating whale sharks and sleek manta rays.

△ *The whale shark is the largest fish in the sea, reaching over 15 metres and weighing over 15 tonnes. It is found off the ribbon reefs of the outer barrier. This 'little' whale shark of four metres lazes just under the surface of the blue reef waters. In spite of their great size whale sharks are harmless to humans, and feed on minute planktonic crustaceans and small fishes.*

△ ◁ *The tiger shark is a large animal that has a bad and thoroughly deserved reputation, for it is a scavenger that will take anything, large or small. It reaches over a tonne in weight, and close to five metres in length. Divers on the reef have little to fear from most sharks, but if a tiger shark is seen it is wise to leave the water! The slanted teeth are razor sharp. Male tigers, like many sharks, have a pair of grooved claspers for transmitting sperm, and insert one or both into the female at mating. A large number of vigorous young are born, fully toothed and capable of looking after themselves at birth.*

Banana fish, *Caesio pisang*

Yellowfin damselfish, *Glyphidodontops flavipinnus*

Blue devil, *Glyphidodontops cyaneus*

△ *The damselfish are perhaps the most obvious and abundant small fishes on the reef, often swimming in small schools of half a dozen, sometimes in scores, and sometimes in hundreds. Many, like this little blue and yellow beauty, hover over or between corals. It is unfortunately named the blue devil but there is nothing devilish about this fish – a harmless, pretty blue damsel.*

△△ *The banana fish is a sleek swimmer. This is more to escape from its predators in midwater than to chase the slow-swimming or drifting planktonic animals on which it feeds.*

▷△ *There are 200 forms of damselfish and over 50 have been found on the Great Barrier Reef. The yellowfin damsel was not known until 1974, and was first collected and named on the reef.*

Blue tang, *Paracanthurus hepatus*

Black-lined Maori wrasse, *Cheilinus diagrammus*

Red emperor, *Lutjanus sebae*

False cleaner, *Plageotremus rhinorhynchos*

Spotted sweetlips, *Plectorhynchus chaetodontoides*

◁ *Surgeonfish got their name from the sharp 'scalpel' that they have at the base of the tail. They have small teeth, sometimes more like bristles, and are algal feeders scraping the surface of the dead coral rock. There are probably two dozen or more species on the reef, from fish with sail-like dorsals, Zebrasoma; unicorn fish with their sharp pointed spike or large blunt bulb, Naso; to many typical surgeons or tangs. One of the most colourful is the blue tang, whose lovely colour, dark blue pattern and yellow tail make it a bright sight against the coral. The scalpel is sheathed, and is not visible in this fish.*

A myriad variety

'In a brief swim along the reef a hundred or so species of fishes, of all shapes, sizes and colours, can be seen.'

Δ *Some small blennies mimic the cleaner wrasse. They do this by looking much the same, and performing a similar dance. Fishes go to them expecting the comfortable grooming of their usual cleaner – instead the false cleaner rushes at them and takes a solid bite of fin or skin. Some species, such as the false cleaner, Aspidontis, have huge lower canine teeth. This false cleaner lacks the huge canines, but still manages to exact its pound of flesh. It has also been known to bite swimmers.*

ΔΔ *One of the most abundant groups on the reef are the wrasses and tuskfish of the Labridae family. They are usually predators, and may be small or large. The black-lined Maori wrasse is a common and typical wrasse but larger than many, reaching one metre in length. Its relative, the giant Maori wrasse, Cheilinus undulatus, grows to over two metres in length.*

Δ *The spotted sweetlips is plain in colour with hexagonal spots as an adult, but the juvenile is a gay creature, with large fins and a strong pattern breaking up the normal fish shape. The adults are large and slow-moving.*

ΔΔ *The small red emperor has an alternative name 'government bream' – an allusion to the red arrows on prison garb. As an adult this pattern is absent or faint. The family of the true snappers, to which the red emperor belongs, has many fish species that are sought for food – the red emperor being one of the most popular. The young may be found in mangrove channels but the adult is a fish of the reef and is commonly seen by divers.*

▷ *Many of the surgeonfish feed in schools, sometimes of more than one species of surgeon, and sometimes even mixing with parrotfish. The blue-lined surgeonfish forms large schools in some places, but in other areas is a solitary species. It is one of the prettiest of surgeons, eagerly sought after as an aquarium species.*

▽ *The butterfly fish, Chaetodontidae, and the angelfish, Pomacanthidae, are to many the typical fishes of the reef. Brightly coloured and highly visible, they are easily recognisable by strong colour patterns. These black-backed butterfly fish can be abundant on the reefs. They do not seem to be strongly territorial, and may be found singly or in groups of various sizes. This pair are swimming with the regal angelfish. The two groups are closely related, but the angelfish has a strong spine at the corner of the gill.*

Blue-lined surgeonfish, *Acanthurus lineatus*

Angelfish, *Pygoplites diacanthus*; butterfly fish, *Chaetodon melannotus*

Emperor angelfish, *Pomacanthus imperator*

Semicircle angelfish, *Pomacanthus semicirculatus*

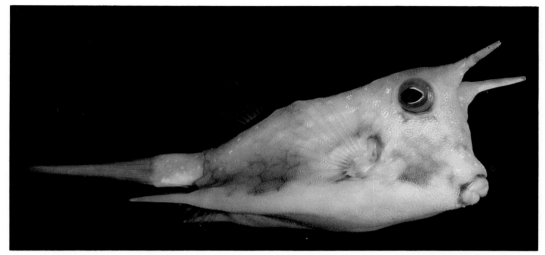

The cowfish or boxfish are encased in armour – a set of fused bony plates that is completely rigid, leaving only the fins and mouth movable. They swim effectively, but slowly, with the pectoral or side fins whirring away. This group of fishes produces a toxic mucus from the skin. Strong horns, a box-like body and a skin toxin should make the species safe from predation but these can apparently be overcome by strong stomachs and the long-horned cowfish is sometimes eaten by large predators. A close relative of this species, the thornback cowfish, Lactoria fornasini, has been studied in Japan and has a strange spawning, with the little male having a number of mates, and spawning with all of them each evening in the spring. After the male has raced around a female for a few moments flashing bright colours, the pair swim up close to the surface; then the male hums to the female, with a hum loud enough to be heard by a diver. After a short nuptial song the cowfish spawn.

Long-horned cowfish, *Lactoria cornutus*

Clown triggerfish, *Balistoides conspicillum*

Meyer's butterfly fish, *Chaetodon meyeri*

△ *The patterns of the clown triggerfish are so distinctive, and so obvious under water and unlike camouflage, that one can only conclude that the fish is advertising that it is poisonous. The colouring seems amazingly detailed, almost making the triggerfish clown-like but the species name given to this fish would suggest that 'conspicuous triggerfish' would be a better common name.*

◁ *The adult emperor angelfish, far left, has a striking colour pattern with masked face and longitudinal yellow lines. The colours of the young are quite different, with concentric circles of white and blue. The adult semicircle angelfish has no mask, although it is beautiful with fine spotting over the body and blue-edged fins, gill covers and spines. Semicircle angels, left, are solitary as adults, but the emperor is often in pairs or threes. Smaller angelfish live in harems with one male and several females.*

Valentin's pufferfish, *Canthigaster valentini*

△ *Meyer's butterfly fish is a bizarre little fish with elaborate stripes. It is not common, but has been found at Heron Island and other places on the reef, in about ten metres of water.*

◁ *A common but shy fish, Valentin's pufferfish live in small territories that are guarded by the females – a number of which are overseen by a male.*

Colour and form
'Like the birds of the air, the coral reef fishes glide over and above their coral caves and turreted coral castles.'

Blue and gold angelfish, *Centropyge bicolor*

Territory and defence

Many coral reef fishes are very territorial. Small fishes, like some of the damsels, will rush at any comers, even large fishes or a diver, and act aggressively to try to keep them off the areas they claim as their own. Usually this is most fiercely done against their own species because members of one species have the same food and space needs.

One of the most interesting examples of territorial behaviour is that of the blue and gold angelfish, *Centropyge bicolor* – a vegetable feeder that lives in groups of four to seven fishes. They prefer portions of reef with algae-covered rubble, and each group has a joint territory that the male defends against other groups. There is usually only one male in this family but when the male dies the largest female changes sex.

While the male's little harem feeds and produces young, he has the task of patrolling the borders of his territory against the surrounding families.

A good strong male can guard enough territory to attract females and keep the group properly fed and therefore reproducing well. Also, weaker males would not be so successful in holding territory and breed less, so that the genes of the stronger males continue in the species, and weak genes disappear. The limited territory defended by the male may be important to the control of population. Instead of sharing food and getting poor nutrition in times of high population numbers, good conditions are provided for the number of fishes the area can feed. Fishes forced into less suitable areas are likely to have poorer nutrition and be more prone to predation and disease. Their family groups could be expected to breed less successfully, reducing the population to a lower level.

△ *The blue and gold angelfish is fiercely territorial to others of its species. The male controls a territory of a few square metres in which he may live with up to seven smaller females. Often there are no other males in his territory, and he rules his small harem like a despot, visiting his females a number of times during the day, patrolling the border of his territory, making sure no surrounding families enter to feed, and preventing any males from capturing or mating with his females. Sometimes his territory may contain a 'bachelor male' who does not breed with his harem. The male mates chiefly in the summer months and, starting 30 minutes before sunset, will usually mate with all the females in turn. If the dominant male is killed (or removed to another spot by a scientist!) the largest female changes sex rapidly, and becomes a fully functional male. If there is a bachelor male, he may take over the harem.*

Black-backed butterfly fish, *Chaetodon melannotus*

◁ *The black-backed butterfly fish seems to show little territorial behaviour and during the day swims over a large area, usually called a 'home range', which it shares with others of the same species. At night it will go to its own resting place deep in the coral, but even here may be near others. This is quite different behaviour from some of its close relatives, such as the strongly territorial chevroned butterfly fish.*

◁ ▽ *The threadfin butterfly fish does not seem to be territorial during the day, but at night expects to sleep in its own spot, and beware any fish that gets in the way. It is able to chase away a medium-sized rock cod (large enough to make a meal of it) by moving backwards into its face with the strong spines of its anal fin erect.*

Black-backed butterfly fish, *Chaetodon melannotus*

△ *A group of black-backed butterfly fish feeds peacefully over the home range. This beautiful creature is common on the Great Barrier Reef.*

Territoriality reduces fighting among the members of species, for the border battles are usually a matter of posturing with no active fighting that could result in injury or death. Each individual knows the borders and will only fight if a neighbour strays into its territory.

All this makes good sense to the individuals concerned in their battle for survival – they each control a set of females by their control of territory, they establish relations with surrounding males which defines their territory without deadly battles or too much waste of energy and there is no surplus of males, for they transform from the females when needed.

Threadfin butterfly fish, *Chaetodon auriga*

▽ A few damselfish farm a small territory, removing the larger algae, and leaving the smaller algae that they prefer to eat. This one-spot damsel removes large algae from its 'farm'. The algae it prefers are more productive and more palatable, and its weeding out of the bigger algae increases its food source. This behaviour is amazingly advanced for a fish.

Bennett's pufferfish, *Canthigaster bennetti*

One-spot damselfish, *Glyphidodontops unimaculatus*

Damselfish, *Glyphidodontops rollandi*

Territoriality, like almost all other behavioural patterns on the reef, is extremely varied. One variation is for females to control their own subterritories within the larger 'family holding' defended by the male. The male patrols the territories of a few females, keeping other males out, and sometimes trying to steal a female and its territory from a neighbour. This happens in the delightful little striped pufferfish, *Canthigaster valentini*. But in crowded areas the territorial system can break down, and the fishes live in a big group where larger fishes are dominant.

Fish farming

Some of the grazing damselfish hold a territory, and actually 'farm' the algae in it. And some species including the damselfish, *Hemiglyphidodon plagiometopon*, defend a small territory that they modify by tearing at the larger tufted algae and

removing them from the territory. They also keep out other grazers, and the result is a managed algal turf, kept strictly for the benefit of individuals of one species.

The home range

But territory is not always so clearly defined. Some of the little butterfly fish will travel over an area that may be ten metres in diameter but not defend it in any strictly territorial sense. Other fishes of different species are ignored, and individuals of the same species may not be chased unless they come very close, when usually the larger fish will briefly chase the smaller. These home ranges, as they are called, may be covered many times a day, and the fishes know them well for food and shelter.

Not all butterfly fish have home ranges. A few species actively defend a territory, and this has been tested in a field experiment. If a territorial species is

△ Two beautiful young damsels face each other in an aggressive encounter over the coral. Many damsels are territorial, and they are most aggressive to their own species – with good reason, for they compete more directly for food and mate with their own kind. Their behaviour is similar to most territorial animals on land and in the sea. Although real fights may occur, once territory is established and boundaries between two territories are learnt, the ritual 'fights' of these little fish are to reconfirm their rights, not to damage each other.

△△ Two Bennett's puffers skirmish at the border between their territories, but such fights are more a statement of position than a battle.

Harlequin tuskfish, *Choerodon fasciatus*

Coral trout, *Plectropomus leopardus*

△ *Two large coral trout communicate closely, but as this species is not strongly territorial the reason is not obvious. This species is known to spawn in groups at particular places on the reef, and it is possible that this confrontation is over an issue of food or space. Individuals of this species may be seen in one area for days or months, and then move off. Tagging has also shown that they may move many kilometres from one reef to another.*

△ △ *One of the wrasses, the harlequin tuskfish, strongly states its territorial position. The harlequin has a clearly defined territory, but is tolerant of large human swimmers, and its beautiful colours can easily be closely observed.*

shown its own image it will get furiously excited, so scientists have painted little wooden models with the colours of a strongly territorial species (like the chevroned butterfly fish, *Chaetodon trifascialis*) and species that are not strongly territorial (like the black-backed butterfly fish, *Chaetodon melannotus*). Placed at the end of a perspex rod and moved slowly towards the chevroned butterfly fish, the little fish will make short rushes towards its image, finally striking it repeatedly with lowered head and dorsal fin spines erect. The spines strike the model, and the bumps can be felt by the holder at the end of the rod. The fish is not deterred even if it loses scales in the process. In contrast the black-backed butterfly fish will simply be curious, and a little crowd of fishes will gather around the model, just looking. Another experimental method is to put a fish in a jam jar with a gauze top, and move it closer or further from the fish being tested.

Territorial fishes will attack the jar furiously as it is placed closer to their territory.

Often fishes that are not normally territorial become so during the breeding season. Some of the big triggerfish of the Balistidae family will migrate to the outer edge of the Great Barrier Reef, and in their hundreds will make shallow depressions in which they lay eggs. The nesting site is then fiercely guarded against all comers.

Seeing the differences

Underlying the territoriality is the importance of vision. Individuals of the same species are recognised visually, and presumably the blue and gold angelfish sees the difference between its family group and a neighbour. Recognition may not only be how the other fish 'looks', but also how it reacts and moves. While feeding, two butterfly fish, many of which pair for life, may temporarily lose each other. One will then rise above the coral and its mate will swim rapidly to it. All this is totally visual, although other clues, such as sounds and scents, are probably sometimes involved.

Migratory movements

Many species have large foraging areas, which may vary with time and cannot be called home ranges. Some of the true snappers, like the yellow-banded hussar, *Lutjanus amabilis*, will school in the same place each day, and then hunt over wide areas at night, even swimming some kilometres. A large coral trout may stay about an area of coral for weeks, or even months, and then move off somewhere else where the feeding is better. The coral trout seems to be opportunistic, and has no close links to any particular place.

Although little is known about the movements of many species, we do know that larger migrations are common among species such as the 'mackerel' of the genus *Scomberomorus*, including the famous Queensland mackerel, *Scomberomorus commerson* – one of the most sought-after game and food fishes on the reef. Such species may make migrations, presumably for spawning, of hundreds of kilometres. In parts of the world (for example the East African island of Zanzibar), the movements of one of the mackerels is well known to fishermen, who trap them on their migrations.

Off Lizard Island Research Station in the northern Great Barrier Reef there are evenings when a large hammerhead shark, *Sphyrna zygaena*, patrols in shallow water up and down off a particular beach. Its appearance seems to be seasonal, and it has been seen for many years. Little is known about the behaviour of such large beasts but it is possible that they develop regular haunts to which they return again and again.

Long migrations demand good navigation skills, and it seems that fishes that migrate thousands of kilometres may have an ability to use the sun and have the necessary sense of time. □

A protected haven

'At the first hint of danger the clowns dart for safety into an anemone from where they grin at a would-be predator suddenly confronted by a barrage of deadly stinging tentacles.'

▷ *This pair of anemone fish are the true 'clown fish' and have a very distinctive waving, dancing, swimming motion. The purpose of this advertising display is still unclear; however they seldom venture far from the protection of their anemone, into which they quickly retreat at the first sign of danger.*

Anemone fish, *Amphiprion chrysopterus*

△ *Anemone fish are among the most strikingly coloured and interesting of coral reef fishes. Although members of the large family of damselfish, Pomacentridae, the anemone fish have evolved the distinctive ability to nestle with impunity among the otherwise poisonous tentacles of sea anemones. This anemone fish is completely unharmed by the stinging cells of the Radianthus anemone in which it is nestling – but another fish would be stung to death.*

Clown anemone fish, *Amphiprion percula*

Clown anemone fish, *Amphiprion percula*

Anemone fish, *Amphiprion perideraion*

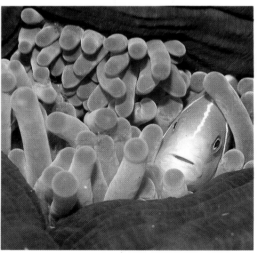

Anemone fish, *Amphiprion perideraion*

△ The distinctive colour pattern and swimming motion of the clown anemone fish make it one of the most noticeable of the fishes on the reef.

◁ This anemone fish is very common and is usually found with the large anemone, Radianthus rilleri. If the anemone is disturbed sufficiently, it will retract all its tentacles and close tightly; the fish will try to escape this potential threat, while keeping a wary eye open.

◁◁ If the anemone is further distressed it will close completely, thus excluding the anemone fish which show distinct signs of distress. Not good swimmers, they quickly fall prey to larger predators when removed from the anemone's protection. Anemone fish are never found without an anemone, but anemones are often found alone.

Lemon-peel angelfish, *Centropyge flavissimus*

Lemon-peel angelfish, *Centropyge flavissimus*

Orange epaulette surgeonfish, *Acanthurus olivaceus*

△ *False eyes are common forms of defence in juvenile fishes (and in butterflies) but are generally located near the tail end of the animal. The reason for this is supposed to be to direct a predator's attack to the fish's rear end where it 'thinks' the head is, thus allowing the fish to escape, often with no more than a few torn tail filaments. But the juvenile lemon-peel angelfish, top, has the false eye in the middle of its body and there is no satisfactory explanation for this paradox.*

▷ *The orange epaulette surgeonfish has a bright yellow juvenile, above right, that is presumed to be a mimic of some of the yellow angelfish that have tougher skin than surgeonfish and a strong spine on the cheek to deter would-be predators.*

Orange epaulette surgeonfish, *Acanthurus olivaceus*

Black and white sea perch, *Macolor niger*

△ *Sea perch, snappers and bass do not often noticeably change colour as they grow but there are two exceptions. One is the red emperor that is generally reddish pink all over but bright red and white as a juvenile, when it is known as the government bream. The other is the black and white sea perch. The juvenile is attractively dressed in a black and white suit which is replaced in the adult, left, by a speckled grey and white pattern, becoming almost sooty grey depending on the fish's mood.*

Black and white sea perch, *Macolor niger*

Changing identity
'Each species of fish has a colour pattern, as unique to that creature as our faces and fingerprints are to us.'

Weedy scorpion fish, *Rhinopias frondosa*

△ *Although distantly related to the stonefish, this weedy scorpion fish, as its scientific name implies, relies on its imitation fronds as camouflage for protection. It is also quite likely that this camouflage helps it to sneak up on unsuspecting prey which it then engulfs with a rapid suction caused by quickly opening its mouth. The jaws and sharp pointy teeth are well suited to its carnivorous ways. The related lionfish also feeds in this manner. The two white spots on the cheeks of the weedy scorpion fish look like eyes when the fish is seen head-on; the real eyes are the little black specks above these white spots.*

Green leatherjacket

◁ *Camouflage is essential for the survival of many fishes – especially the young that are less able than adults to defend themselves or escape predators. Smaller individuals will always have more potential predators than larger ones. Many have therefore evolved both colour patterns and special shapes to blend with their surroundings. The juvenile filefish or leatherjacket is green with a circular shape that makes it appear very similar to a blade of seaweed – which can be seen below and to the left of the fish. The skin is also covered with fine projections of a grey colour which copy the filamentous algae and sediment attached to the seaweeds.*

▷ *Many fishes mimic weeds, leaves and other fishes, but few actually mimic the corals in which they live. The exception is the coral blenny that lives among* Pocillopora *corals and feeds on filamentous algae.*

Peacock sole, *Pardachirus pavoninus*

◁ The peacock sole, like most of the flat fishes of the sole family, is a master of camouflage, and can change its colour to match its surroundings, and its pattern to match the type of sea bed on which it likes to settle. The camouflage is enhanced by the practice of fluffing up some of the sand when it comes to rest, as the sand then drifts back over the fish making it almost invisible. These little fish have still another trick. At the base of the spines of the dorsal fin are numerous glands which secrete a milky toxin which is ejected if they are eaten. Experiments with sharks in the Red Sea have shown that this secretion is extremely distasteful to the sharks which spit out the fish before any harm has come to it. Scientists are now investigating the possibility of using this as a natural shark repellent for human use.

Anglerfish, *Antennarius*

△ This anglerfish lives among sponges. Its pectoral fins are modified into little walking legs and its first dorsal fin spine is elongated with a tassel on its end looking like a worm. This fishing rod and lure is dangled in front of the mouth to entice unsuspecting fishes to come to examine the bait — and suddenly find themselves inside its mouth.

Coral blenny, *Exallias brevis*

The ultimate mimics

'Fishes may imitate weeds, stony algae, coral or each other to survive. Juveniles of two species may be look-alikes and school together, and their adults be different and live apart.'

Fairy basslet, *Anthias*

△ *In this example of mimicry between a fairy basslet and a hawkfish, right, the fairy basslet is not poisonous or toxic but has some degree of protection from predation because of its schooling behaviour. The hawkfish joins in with these schools hovering off the front of reefs and has adapted its feeding to be like that of the fairy basslets, eating plankton rather than feeding on invertebrates from the bottom of the sea like most other hawkfish.*

A clever copy

'In many museum collections throughout the world a fish and its mimic can be found in the same bottle with the same label – even the experts are fooled!'

Hawkfish, *Cyprinocirrhites polyactis*

Striped toby, *Canthigaster valentini*

Pearl-scaled angelfish, *Centropyge vroliki*

Surgeonfish, *Acanthurus*

Leatherjacket, *Paraluteres prionurus*

△ There are several examples of juvenile surgeonfish mimicking angelfish. The pearl-scaled angelfish, top, is the model for the juvenile surgeonfish of an unknown species.

◁ Toadfish and pufferfish, belonging to the family Tetraodontidae, are among the most poisonous of all marine creatures. They possess a powerful nerve poison called tetraodotoxin that is toxic to other fish predators and may produce a rapid and violent death in humans. The little striped toby, above left, is one of the more common puffers to be found around coral reefs, and is almost indistinguishable from its leatherjacket mimic. The similarity in colour patterns is perhaps the best example of mimicry in the fish world. The leatherjacket is not in the least toxic. The only successful way to tell them apart is by the shape of the soft dorsal fin — the striped toby has a short stumpy dorsal fin placed well down on the back, while the leatherjacket has a long transparent dorsal fin along most of its back.

Marine reptiles: creatures of habit

Reef turtles

There are few more memorable events in nature than the laborious egg-laying ritual of the sea turtles that nest in great numbers on islands of the reef.

During the peak breeding season, from October to February (and less frequently at other times of year), the female turtles come ashore to lay their eggs while the males cruise offshore in the hope of mating with the females in transit. The patterns of egg-laying behaviour vary in subtle ways between the six species that breed in reef waters. Three of these – the green turtle, *Chelonia mydas*, the loggerhead, *Caretta caretta*, and the hawksbill, *Eretmochelys imbricata* – nest mainly on coral cays. The flatback turtle, *Chelonia depressa*, nests principally on several continental islands and sometimes, like the green turtle and loggerhead turtle, on the mainland. The leatherback or luth, *Dermochelys coriacea*, seldom nests in Australia, although it sometimes passes along the reef in its southward migration. The Pacific ridley, *Lepidochelys olivacea*, is a rare visitor to reef waters.

All six, however, have much in common, especially the lumbering emergence of the female from the sea and its exploration of the beach above high-water mark. There the turtle may make several false starts at nest building, leaving behind a series of large depressions in the sand. When it has settled on a suitable site the turtle hollows out a depression in the sand by gradually pivoting its body while using its flippers, mainly the front ones, to throw sand aside in a seemingly haphazard way. Eventually, the whole body lies within this large hollow. With cupped hind flippers the turtle then carefully scoops out a hole about 200 millimetres in diameter and 400 millimetres deep, in which is laid – varying with the species – from about 50 to 150 round, soft-shelled eggs that closely resemble ping-pong balls. The female turtle may deposit three to five such clutches in any one season. When each egg is laid it has a shallow depression in one side that rounds out in a few days as quite a strong pressure develops in the egg. After egg-laying the turtle fills in the nest and, moving forwards, throws sand about with its front flippers to obscure the site.

On many islands this process is undertaken by dozens or even hundreds of turtles in a single night. On uninhabited islands, however, the numbers may

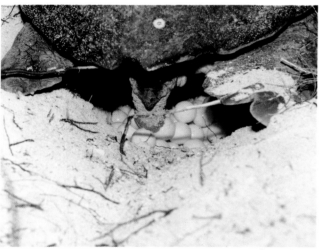

Turtle egg chamber

△ *The back of an egg chamber has been dug away to reveal the eggs being laid. The number of eggs in a single clutch may range from 50 to 150, the higher numbers usually being laid by larger, older females nesting for the first time in a season. The eggs in a single clutch are not laid continuously, but in small groups over a period of up to about half an hour.*

▷ *On the way from their nest to the sea these newly hatched green turtles run the risk of being eaten by predatory ghost crabs. The distinctive colour pattern – black above and white below – will soon change to the beautiful variegated pattern characteristic of the adult green turtle, while the shell, which is soft and leathery at hatching, will quickly harden.*

Green turtle, *Chelonia mydas*

Loggerhead turtle, *Caretta caretta*

Female turtle track

be much greater: more than 10 000 female turtles have been recorded emerging to nest in a single night on Raine Island in a good season. The numbers may be greater than an island's capacity to hold them, and the only way the turtles can find a nest site is to dig up an existing nest. Equally large numbers of turtles may nest nearly every night for weeks at a time.

Researchers differ in their estimates of how long it takes before a female turtle is sexually mature and lays her first clutch of eggs. For the green turtle, estimates range from ten to more than 40 years.

Survival of the hatchlings

After they have been laid the eggs develop over the next six or seven weeks until the fully formed babies almost completely fill the eggs. At this stage their shells are soft and their bodies are folded in the middle, so that they are rolled up rather like an armadillo. The eggs in the nest tend to hatch at about the same time, except those that are infertile or fail to develop. When hatching occurs during the day, the young usually remain within the nest until dark. They then scramble up through the sand and set off for the sea. Their sense of direction can be upset by distractions such as lights from buildings or beacons, but their ability to home in on the sea, even when it lies behind sand ridges or can't be heard, is usually unfailing and has for a long time confounded biologists.

On their way to the water's edge the baby turtles run the gauntlet of predatory crabs. If, by some error of judgement, the turtles emerge during the day, then seagulls and other birds swoop on many before they reach the water. Hatchling mortality is greatest on mainland beaches where other predators, especially foxes, pigs and goannas, abound. Even when they reach the safety of the sea, few baby turtles will ever reach maturity.

Incubation and sex

Recent research indicates that the incubation temperature affects the sex of turtles. Previously, the sex of each embryo was thought to be genetically predetermined, until it was found that clutches of eggs incubated at different temperatures could produce either all males or all females. Further experimental work has shown that nests incubated at an average temperature of about 30° Centigrade produce approximately equal numbers of males and females. As the incubation temperature drops towards 26° Centigrade, males predominate, while above 30° Centigrade females begin to outnumber males. Within this temperature range various proportions of males and females are produced.

Slow and steady travellers

Over the past 20 years thousands of hatchlings and adults on the Great Barrier Reef have been tagged. This has provided much information on the distances turtles travel – sometimes over 1000 kilometres in a

△ *The track of a female turtle is distinctive. Emergent and return tracks can be identified by the position of the sand that piles up behind the flippers, and by the central tail track that tends to be continuous on the return (downhill) run to the water but appears as a series of finger-like depressions on the emergent track where the tail is pushed into the sand.*

△ ◁ *A female loggerhead turtle makes a nesting hollow. The front flippers have been used to excavate the hollow by throwing sand backwards in wide arcs, while the turtle turns its body and moves forward to increase the size of the pit. When this is done the turtle uses its hind flippers to excavate a smaller hole for the eggs.*

single year. But because researchers have ready access to turtles at only two stages of their life cycle – when they hatch and when adult females return to island beaches to lay their eggs – knowledge of their life histories is fragmentary. Little is known about what turtles do between hatching and maturity. And because male turtles do not leave the sea, most of our information about turtles is based on females.

All of the available evidence suggests that turtles generally return to breed on the islands where they were born. Turtle canneries that operated in Queensland earlier this century made inroads into regional breeding populations of the green turtle. More recent attempts to 'farm' turtles in

Green turtle, *Chelonia mydas*

Torres Strait, while politically popular, have been an ecological failure. Today, turtles can be taken for food only by Aborigines and Torres Strait islanders, and are otherwise protected by law from man.

Vegetarians and carnivores

Of the six species of sea turtles found in Great Barrier Reef waters, the green turtle of turtle soup fame, and the less common loggerhead, are found throughout the world's tropical seas. The green turtle is largely vegetarian as an adult, feeding on a variety of marine plants, while the more heavily built loggerhead is carnivorous, feeding mainly on molluscs and fishes.

The only sea turtle confined to the Australian region is the flatback. Its shell is more flattened than in other species, usually with the edges turned upwards in adults. It, too, is carnivorous with crustaceans favoured as food.

Although very common throughout the reef, and the smallest of our marine turtles, the hawksbill breeds mostly on only a few northern islands. Also a carnivore, its shell was once highly sought after to be polished and made into combs and jewellery. As its name implies, the hawksbill turtle has a projecting, parrot-like upper jaw.

While more commonly encountered elsewhere in Australia, two other turtles are occasionally seen in Great Barrier Reef waters. These are the Pacific ridley, which superficially resembles the flatback, but with a higher shell, and the giant leatherback or luth. The luth reaches nearly two metres in length and may weigh as much as a tonne. Whereas other sea turtles have a continuous bony carapace with a horny covering, the shell of the luth consists of numerous small polygonal bony plates imbedded in a leathery skin. Despite its enormous size it feeds mainly on jellyfish and salps.

△ *An adult green turtle swims over a reef, where it forages for sea grasses and algae. Although green turtles surface about every ten to thirty minutes for air, they can stay submerged for many hours at a time if necessary and will often rest underwater in crevices or below overhanging coral shelves.*

Crocodiles and sea snakes

While turtles are by far the most common marine reptiles encountered on the Great Barrier Reef, two other reptilian groups – crocodiles and sea snakes – may sometimes be seen. The saltwater crocodile, *Crocodylus porosus*, does venture out to sea and may arrive at a Great Barrier Reef island, but this happens so rarely that visitors to the reef need not feel at risk. Sea snakes are much more likely to be seen by people snorkelling or scuba diving.

Sea snakes are by nature shy and inoffensive in the water but have acquired a fearsome reputation from their aggressive behaviour when they have been dragged from the water in a net or on a fishing line. One sea snake in particular – the olive sea snake, *Aipysurus laevis* – seems to have an innate curiosity that often brings it into contact with a diver. Unlike other sea snakes, which will usually ignore or move away from an approaching diver, the olive sea snake will sometimes head straight for a diver, twining itself about limbs, body or speargun. This can be a terrifying experience; the snake's venom is lethal and in attempting to dislodge the snake a diver runs the risk of making it bite. Fortunately, the fangs of the olive sea snake, like those of most sea snakes, are quite short and only the largest specimens can bite through a wet suit.

Sea snakes have been found to possess some of the most potent animal toxins known, although there is much variation between species. One snake that is common in Great Barrier Reef waters, the turtle-headed sea snake, *Emydocephalus annulatus*, has evolved the habit of feeding only on fish eggs and in the process has virtually lost its fangs, teeth and venom glands. Some other sea snakes feed exclusively on burrowing eels and have evolved a body that allows them to reach deep inside burrows for their prey; the head and front third of their bodies are thin and eel-like, whereas the hind part of the body is much deeper.

Most sea snakes, however, feed on a variety of fishes – some even eat poisonous fishes. About 12 of the 30 species of sea snake found in Australian waters are found on the Great Barrier Reef. All share a number of features that are wonderful adaptations to life in the sea. They have paddle-shaped tails to help propel them through the water and valved nostrils that seal their air passages when they are submerged. Sea snakes are air-breathing reptiles and must come to the surface to breathe. Most replenish their air supply about every 20 to 30 minutes, but if necessary can stay submerged for up to an hour or more.

The potent neurotoxic venoms possessed by many sea snakes have probably evolved in response to the special conditions of life in the sea. Land snakes can use their outstanding olfactory powers to follow the trail of an animal which, having been bitten, moves some distance before dying. But unless a fish bitten by a sea snake dies almost instantly, it may escape into a coral crevice, or be eaten by another animal. In the meantime, the moving water prevents the snake from picking up the victim's scent.

Externally, female sea snakes are usually indistinguishable from males. In most species, however, the females have shorter tails, and in those species with rough or spiny scales the spines are much better developed in the males.

Most sea snakes in Australian waters belong to a group in which between two and ten live young are produced at sea. Most are helpless on land, with only a few species coming ashore, and then only to bask on mud flats or among mangroves. Occasionally, however, one may come across a sea krait, *Laticauda*. The sea kraits are found on many Pacific islands, as well as in New Guinea and countries of Southeast Asia. They are not livebearing, but produce eggs; they are usually brilliantly marked with alternate black and pale blue bands, and move about easily on land where they also lay their eggs.

Sea snakes are common in some areas but rarely seen in others, although the reasons for their patchy distribution are not fully understood. There have been a number of unconfirmed reports throughout the tropical Indo-Pacific region of large groups of sea snakes forming floating islands of thousands of intertwined individuals.□

Turtle-headed sea snake, *Emydocephalus annulatus*

△ *A brilliantly banded specimen of the turtle-headed sea snake, a harmless species that feeds only on the eggs of burrowing blennies and gobies. Most species have far less colour, usually being black or dark brown with only a few pale spots or blotches. Like all of the true sea snakes, it bears live young in the sea.*

◁ *The olive sea snake is one of the most common sea snakes encountered in clear, shallow reef waters, where it is often attracted to divers, much to their consternation! It is highly venomous, its bite quickly immobilising the fish on which it feeds. However, it is not aggressive, and it will rarely bite a swimmer or diver unless molested.*

'Large groups of sea snakes form floating islands of thousands of intertwined individuals.'

Olive sea snake, *Aipysurus laevis*

Humpback whale, *Megaptera novaeangliae*

134 LIFE ABOVE AND AMONG CORALS

Marine mammals: gargantuan yet graceful

Whales and dolphins

No one can fail to be awed by the gargantuan might of a whale or captivated by the agile grace of a dolphin. Yet the whales and dolphins of the Great Barrier Reef are a paradox. Although this group includes the largest and most popular animals that occur in reef waters, very little is known about them. It is also ironic that this knowledge has come mostly from the study of the sometimes putrid carcasses of animals that have been stranded on beaches, have been accidentally drowned after becoming tangled in nets, or have been killed by man for oil, meat and other products.

Whales and dolphins are warm-blooded and belong to the order Cetacea which is divided into two distinct subgroups: Mysticeti, commonly known as baleen or whalebone whales, and Odontoceti, the toothed whales. The baleen or whalebone whales strain their small prey from the water by means of horny 'whalebone' plates called 'baleen' which fringe the upper jaw. In contrast, toothed whales are active predators that catch fishes, squid and other prey and swallow them whole.

Ancestral whales evolved from land-dwelling mammals that are thought to have entered shallow seas to take advantage of rich fish stocks. Deposited in river sediments about 53 million years ago, the skull of *Pakicetus*, the oldest whale yet discovered, has teeth that are not only similar to those of primitive whales, but also resemble those of mesonychid Condylarthra, strange, hooved, wolf-like terrestrial mammals that are now extinct. The skull of *Pakicetus* indicates that it was not fully aquatic because its earbones have features of both terrestrial mammals and modern whales, whose hearing systems have been modified through evolution to pick up sounds travelling through water.

Today's whales and dolphins are highly adapted to spend their entire lives in the water. Typical mammalian features that were not useful or essential in their aquatic environment – such as a lot of hair, a fully mobile neck, most of the pelvic girdle and the hind limbs – have disappeared. Whales and dolphins have a streamlined fish-like shape and move rapidly through the water propelled by the vertical strokes of their powerful tail flukes; their forelimbs have been modified as paddle-shaped flippers. Many species have a dorsal fin that is important for both control of movement through the water and temperature regulation, especially in the smaller species. Because whales and dolphins are warm-blooded they must maintain their core body temperature within narrow limits. They must also come to the surface to breathe, and in the process of evolution their nostrils have moved to a position high on top of the head to form a single or paired blowhole.

Probably because they are such mobile animals the range of most cetacean species extends over a huge geographical area. Not surprisingly, most of the species that have been recorded in Great Barrier Reef waters are those that are known to occur in relatively shallow, tropical, warm temperate seas for at least part of the year.

The long-distance swimmers

The largest family of whalebone whales is the Balaenopteridae or rorqual. Rorquals have long grooves along their throats which enable them to fill their mouths with huge amounts of water from which the whale sieves planktonic crustaceans or small fishes (depending on the type of whale). The rorqual's soft fleshy tongue is well adapted for licking food from the filtering baleen.

All six species of rorqual have been recorded off the Queensland coast and all are believed to pass through Great Barrier Reef waters. However,

◁ *Humpback mother and calf simultaneously raise their tail flukes as they dive together in the Whitsunday Island area. These whales, photographed in late September, were probably heading south to the Antarctic to spend the summer feeding. Between 1952 and 1962, commercial whaling reduced the population of humpback whales migrating along Australia's east coast from approximately 10 000 to about 200 animals. Recent studies estimate the present number to be about 600 whales and indicate that the population is slowly recovering. However, sightings of humpbacks are still comparatively rare, a far cry from pre-whaling days when fishermen claimed that winter sightings were commonplace in Great Barrier Reef waters.*

▷ *The giant humpback whales, which may grow to over 15 metres, seek the best of both worlds by wintering in the tropics and spending the summer feeding in Antarctic seas. To do this they must migrate thousands of kilometres each year. The Australian east coast humpbacks travel through southern and central Great Barrier Reef waters to unknown tropical breeding grounds. Because humpbacks are known to breed in sheltered waters around reefs and islands in other parts of the world, some scientists now consider it likely that humpbacks breed in Great Barrier Reef waters.*

Humpback whale, *Megaptera novaeangliae*

except for the more coastal species – the humpback and the minke – these giant animals are reported very rarely in the area. Blue, fin, sei and humpback whales migrate regularly, forming large summer feeding schools in Antarctic waters and moving north to breed in warm waters in winter. The humpback whale passes close to the eastern Australian coast on its way north. Bryde's whale appears to be a warm-water species that rarely moves north or south. The minke whales seen in Great Barrier Reef waters during the winter months are distinct from the substantial populations seen in the Antarctic during summer and may belong to a warm-water race.

Whalebone whales are usually sighted alone or in small groups, and the only social unit that has been established definitely is a mother and her calf. However, it is possible that the low-frequency sounds produced by whalebone whales may help to

group includes oceanic species such as pilot whales, beaked whales, killer whales and spinner dolphins, which usually travel some distance from the coast but occasionally come close inshore and may become stranded. The second group consists of three inshore species that frequent bays and estuaries: the bottlenose dolphin, *Tursiops truncatus*, the Irrawaddy River dolphin, *Orcaella brevirostris*, and the Indo-Pacific humpback dolphin, *Sousa chinensis*.

Sociable, toothed whales

On the whole, toothed whales are more gregarious than whalebone whales but there is a wide variation in the social behaviour of different species. The inshore species are usually seen in small groups, and recent field studies in various parts of the world suggest that the composition of bottlenose and Indo-Pacific humpback dolphin schools is changing constantly. Research in Hawaii indicates that the

examined. It was found in the Somali Republic of East Africa. No one is yet certain that they have seen this species alive.

It is not only rare species that are little known. The Irrawaddy River dolphin is common inshore north of Mackay. Although well known to locals, this species was not recorded officially in Australian waters until an American scientist recognised the skulls of two dolphins that had been eaten by Arnhem Land Aborigines in 1948. It was not reported in reef waters until the 1960s.

Identifying cetaceans at sea is often difficult, even for experienced observers. But with the growing interest in whales, more amateur observers are recording, photographing and reporting their sightings, and knowledge of these creatures is increasing gradually. If humpback whales recover to their pre-whaling numbers, watching whales may become a highlight of winter visits to the reef.

Minke whale, *Balaenoptera acutorostrata*

Irrawaddy River dolphin, *Orcaella brevirostris*

maintain contact between animals situated quite a distance from each other.

The most vocal whalebone whale is the humpback, whose repertoire in its tropical habitat is a complex, repeating song. Some studies indicate that humpbacks sing mainly in or near their tropical breeding areas and may be largely silent at other stages of migration. However, along the east coast of Australia, singing humpbacks have been recorded at Coffs Harbour, in New South Wales, at least 1000 kilometres south of their breeding grounds.

The 16 species of toothed whales that occur in the waters of the Great Barrier Reef range in size from the giant sperm whale, the males of which average 15 metres in length, to slender dolphins less than two metres long. The sperm whale is an oceanic species that prefers deep water while the small whales and dolphins form two groups on the basis of their broad ecological requirements. The first

oceanic spinner dolphin occurs in schools of varied size and composition. In contrast, breeding schools of some other oceanic species, such as sperm whales, pilot whales and killer whales, are believed to consist primarily of stable groups of closely related females and their young.

Experiments with several species of captive toothed whales suggests that they can detect prey by echo location. Echo-locating animals scan their environment acoustically by emitting intense series of high-frequency clicks and interpreting the time and direction of their return. Only some of these clicks are audible to the human ear.

Longman's beaked whale, *Indopacetus pacificus*, a toothed whale first discovered in Great Barrier Reef waters, is probably the rarest whale in the world. This species was described from the skull and jaw of a specimen found near Mackay, Queensland, in 1881, and since then only one other skull has been

△ *Irrawaddy River dolphins are often mistaken for dugongs. Both species occur in the coastal waters of the Great Barrier Reef region. The mistake probably arises because Irrawaddy River dolphins, usually less than three metres long, lack the typical beak of better-known species such as the bottlenose dolphin. The easiest way to distinguish an Irrawaddy River dolphin from a dugong is to look for a dorsal fin, which a dugong does not have.*

△ ◁ *Minke whales visit the reef each winter. They are often inquisitive and appear to inspect boats and divers. Swimming with a minke is an exciting experience; however, it is comforting to remember that minke whales, which grow up to ten metres long, have no teeth. Unlike the minkes seen in Antarctic waters each summer, the minke whales that visit the reef waters have distinctive white markings on their flippers and shoulder regions.*

'Dolphins must come to the surface to breathe, and in the process of evolution their nostrils have moved to a position high on top of the head.'

Spinner dolphin, *Stenella longirostris*

◁ *Schools of spinner dolphins, like this one bow-riding a boat on the outer Great Barrier Reef, are common worldwide in warm seas. The spinner dolphin is so-called because of its habit of spinning around on its tail up to four times in the course of a single leap. Some scientists believe that this is done to make noise and may be an important means of communication, especially when animals are dispersed. An oceanic species, the spinner dolphin is slim-bodied and reaches at least two metres in lengh.*

Bottlenose dolphin, *Tursiops truncatus*

△ *Recent research suggests that dolphins swimming near the surface at high speed save energy by leaping. These bottlenose dolphins, photographed leaping in the waters between Townsville and Wheeler Reef, are the species most often kept in oceanaria. Bottlenose dolphins are distributed widely in coastal waters of the Pacific, Atlantic and Indian Oceans and they are common in reef waters where they are often seen riding the bow waves of boats. Adult bottlenose dolphins grow to three metres.*

Indo-Pacific humpback dolphin, *Sousa chinensis*

◁ *The Indo-Pacific humpback dolphin is a rather slow-moving coastal species that is common inshore in Great Barrier Reef waters. It tends to occur in small groups of about six that may spread out to hunt fishes. Humpback dolphins can enter very shallow water and have been observed feeding within a few metres of shore. Adult humpback dolphins are about two metres long.*

Dugong, *Dugong dugon*

△ *Dugongs feed mainly on sea grasses, although algae are often eaten incidentally as well. In Great Barrier Reef waters, dugongs prefer to feed on soft and delicate sea grasses, presumably because they are more nutritious than fibrous species. The whole plant, including the roots and rhizomes, is dug up leaving a serpentine feeding trail in the sea grass bed. The dugong's upper lip area, covered with sensory bristles, is a versatile and complex structure used to grasp the sea grasses and convey them to the mouth. An adult dugong can eat up to 40 kilograms of sea grass a day.*

'The only sounds that have been recorded from captive dugongs are bird-like chirps, rather like those of a budgerigar.'

Dugong, *Dugong dugon*

Dugongs: shy sea cows

The dugong, *Dugong dugon*, is one of only four surviving species of sirenians or sea cows. Its closest relative, the giant eight-metre Steller's sea cow, was exterminated by man in the 18th century. The only other surviving sirenians are the three species of manatee that occur in the Caribbean region, the Amazon and West Africa respectively. Depending on the species, manatees usually spend some or all of their lives in fresh water, whereas the dugong is the only herbivorous mammal that is marine.

Like whales and dolphins, dugongs spend their entire lives in the sea and their bodies show similar adaptations to a life of swimming and diving. Dugongs grow to about three metres and from a distance look rather like dolphins with their fish-like shape, whale-like tail fluke and paddle-shaped flippers. Unlike dolphins, however, dugongs are not active predators. They feed instead on sea grasses that grow in warm, sheltered, shallow inshore waters. As a result, dugongs tend to be bulkier, less streamlined and slower moving than dolphins. They have sparse body hair apart from thick sensory bristles around the mouth; these are believed to be important for detecting suitable food plants.

Unlike cetaceans, dugongs do not seem to be able to communicate over long distances or to echo locate. The only sounds that have been recorded from captive dugongs are bird-like chirps, rather like those of a budgerigar!

Historically, the dugong occurred throughout the tropical and subtropical coastal and island waters of the Indian and west Pacific oceans from East Africa to the Solomon Islands. It is now considered to be rare in most of these areas and vulnerable to extinction. Aerial surveys conducted since the mid-1970s, however, have shown herds (sometimes numbering more than 100 dugongs) in the shallow seas of northern Australia, and it is likely that this region now harbours most of the world's dugongs.

Dugongs occur along the coast or on large flat reefs such as Corbett Reef in Princess Charlotte Bay where they can feed on sea grasses. Up to 600 dugongs have been seen from the air near the mouth of the Starcke River north of Cooktown, making this the most important dugong habitat yet identified in the world.

The age of a dugong can be determined by counting the growth layers in its tusks, which are laid down like the growth rings of a tree. Dugongs live for up to 70 years and females do not bear their first calf until they are at least ten years old; one calf is produced at intervals of three to seven years. Calving, which has been observed only rarely, takes place in very shallow water with the mother aground but in the wash of the waves. The cow-calf bond is well developed, and calves remain with their mothers for at least two years.

Dugongs have long been prized for their delicious meat (which has been likened to veal, beef and pork) and for the medicinal value of their oil. In the 1920s Aborigines netted dugongs in the Starcke River area to obtain oil that was then supplied to Aboriginal communities throughout Queensland.

The dugong was the basis of the whole culture of the sandbeach tribes whose territories extended from Princess Charlotte Bay north almost to Cape York. The dugong hunting practised by these people has been described as undoubtedly the most spectacular occupation of any Australian Aborigine.

Dugongs are now protected in Australia except for subsistence hunting by Aborigines and Torres Strait islanders living in native communities. These people, who usually hunt from an outboard-powered aluminium dinghy, using a harpoon with a detachable head called a *wap*, still regard the dugong as a very important part of their traditions.

The dugong is very vulnerable to over-exploitation because it is such a slow breeder. A major threat to dugongs in Great Barrier Reef waters is their tendency to drown after becoming tangled accidentally in fishing nets. Marine parks and other sanctuaries from which net-fishing is banned, and in which native hunting is regulated, need to be established in important dugong areas; the first of these has been declared at the Starcke River. Without such properly enforced protection the dugong faces extinction. □

◁ ▽ *Although about the size and shape of a rotund dolphin, the dugong is more closely related to the elephant. Adult dugongs are between two and a half and three metres long and weigh from 250 to 400 kilograms. Their skin is very thick and smooth and is often heavily scarred. The nostrils, which are covered with valve-like flaps when the animal is submerged, are close together and situated near the front of the snout so that the dugong can breathe with most of its body below the surface. Dugongs are quiet, gentle animals and because they often occur in muddy waters they are rarely seen by the casual observer.*

▷ *The bond between the female dugong and her calf is strong and long lasting. A single calf is born and may be suckled for up to two years, although it usually starts eating sea grass soon after birth. The mother has two mammary glands, one under each flipper, a position similar to that of human breasts. Despite legendary sailors' tales claiming that the female dugong suckled her calf while upright and half out of the water, modern research has shown that the calf suckles while the mother swims or feeds, apparently taking little notice.*

Dugong, *Dugong dugon*

Mangroves

Part four: humans and the reef

Humans have been involved with the Great Barrier Reef for over 40 000 years. It has been fished for seafoods and searched for shells, and the variety of its marine animals has been wondered at. But as the 21st century approaches our relationship with nature has changed. For the first time our increasing population and our ability to harness huge quantities of energy have enabled us, often not through our own collective wish, to make irreversible changes on a global scale. Will the reef be immune from these changes?

There is no definite answer to this question, but it is likely that the reef will continue to be a 'coral battleground', to use words of the poet Judith Wright. There will be those who will exploit the reef's resources, with no thought for future generations. And there will be those who will strive to keep man away from it altogether, forgetting that it has already come to terms with a thousand generations of humans. Somewhere between these two extremes, man and the reef will eventually achieve a balance.

Early Aboriginal prehistory of the area is still obscure, for much of the archaeological evidence is under reef waters and waits for work by divers. When Europeans first arrived, the Aboriginal coastal people were using huge 20-metre double outrigger canoes in the north of the reef. These were built in Papua and obtained by barter. Further south the Aborigines built smaller canoes, and travelled confidently up and down the reef and to outlying islands. But the early story – lasting tens of thousands of years – will never be fully known. It is likely that those early inhabitants were hardy coastal people, skilful fishermen who caught turtle and dugong as well as fishes and shellfish with fine traps, lines, hooks and spears. In the 18th century there were 40 tribal groups along the coast, living in tune with the coastal and reef environment.

European exploration in the early 19th century started a period of great change, with sailors traversing the intricate coral maze, and the settlement of the north by the new immigrants, spurred on by the discovery of gold. Scores of vessels were wrecked on the reefs until improved charts, towers and lights tamed these waters towards the end of the century.

Conflict was common along the Queensland coast at this time. Murder of Aborigines by whites – with subsequent retaliation – and the spread of European diseases, decimated coastal groups. But Aborigines became an integral part of most maritime industries, including the collecting of shells and bêche-de-mer, and local shipping.

The diving for pearl oyster shells, then later trochus, *Trochus niloticus*, and the green snail shell, *Turbo marmoratus*, all for the making of mother-of-pearl buttons, was an industry occupying many luggers with big crews in the late 19th and early 20th centuries.

Reef use has changed again, and trawl nets are now being used increasingly for prawns, as well as the more traditional handline and trolled lure for fishes. With the growth of tourism, recreational fishermen are now being catered for.

The pursuit of leisure has become the reef's biggest industry, and as this has become more sophisticated, the gentle arts of bird watching, botanising, photography and diving, in order to look and learn, have become popular.

These changes have done little so far to disturb the reef. Perhaps coastal land-use changes and industry may have greater effects in the future, but at present the reef retains a pristine, timeless aura. □

◁ *Mangroves grow in saline soil and adapt themselves to the rise and fall of the tides which submerge their lower branches and leaves in sea water.*

▽ *On 11 June 1770 the* Endeavour *struck a coral reef off the Queensland coast and almost sank. The ship was anchored for repairs in the river now named after it near present-day Cooktown. Two months later, Captain Cook succeeded in sailing through a narrow passage near Lizard Island, only to seek again the protection of the reefs.*

HMS *Endeavour*

Diving and snorkelling: a wilderness adventure

The world of the reef

Since the beginning of time, man has sought new worlds but perhaps one of the strangest to be found is also for many people readily accessible. A journey into the sea requires only a mask and snorkel. With them, one can hover like a bird above the kaleidoscopic pastures of the reef and, for a moment, share that world with its inhabitants.

The Great Barrier Reef is particularly rich and rewarding. It offers the experience of snorkelling in shallow sun-drenched lagoons and the chance to be suspended near a vertical coral wall over waters that drop off to great depths. Colour and drama, movement, contrast, mystery and grandeur are there, but never sameness or boredom. Yet, a visit is not simply an underwater activity: calm turquoise

△ *A reef is more than just a diving adventure; to the underwater photographer, it is an endless array of shapes, colours and patterns that, because of the clear waters, can be captured on film. The camera's flash reveals an extraordinary world of brilliance beyond imagination.*

waters, clear sunny skies, small boats, quiet warm nights amid tropical vegetation, relaxation and a sense of apartness from the daily environment are also what the Great Barrier Reef is about.

Viewing the underwater world of the reef is as easy as floating in a bath. The clarity of the water and the penetration of sunlight ensures that everything there can see the light of day; nothing is hidden or swallowed by the swirling fog of turbid waters.

The shapes are clear and the colours are rich when seen from an underwater observatory or from a glass-bottomed boat. But the true experience of

the reef is a private one. To discover the mystery and excitement of the underwater world one needs to don face-mask and snorkel, and swim down into the silence below; a silence removed from the concrete echoes of the underwater observatory and the squeals from the glass-bottomed boat.

Joining the underwater life

Drifting in the shallows, one can watch the small sand-inhabiting fishes such as flathead, grubfish, gobies, rays and lizard fish dart from their resting places on the sand to settle farther on. Among the corals of the reef flat, the numbers of fishes increase dramatically with blennies, demoiselles and damselfish, and wrasses of all shapes and sizes. The brush-like turtle weed can be seen providing a vivid green home for an equally vivid green crab.

Nearer the reef edge, the profusion increases, seemingly to the point of overcrowding. Large groups of the blue-green pullers shelter in the staghorn gardens, butterfly fish dart to and fro while masses of surgeons, stripey snappers, sweetlips, parrotfish and sergeant majors appear to mill around aimlessly.

With increasing confidence, one can venture down the reef slope, or brave the surf on the windward side of the reef, or dive the reef slope or lagoon at night, when cardinal fish, squirrelfish, moray eels and cuttlefish can be seen on their nocturnal forays. Then, too, other fishes can be approached under ledges or in holes in the reef, or the delicate structure of the coral can be admired or the blinded turtle can be observed at close quarters. The shadowy outlines of even larger predators may also be glimpsed.

Alternately, one can explore a wreck, a slowly dissolving time capsule of a long-gone past, now providing a lodging house for a variety of boarders. Here, one is likely to find pennant coral fish weaving in and out of dark openings, schools of fusiliers hovering above, or large groupers, furtively darting to secret lairs within.

Knowing the reef

These are some of the riches of this underwater world. But the beauty and serenity of the reef can lull the diver into a false sense of security. There are treacherous currents, the coral is sharp, and it is just as easy to be harmed in crystal clear waters as it is in other areas.

Local knowledge is essential for any diving activity on or about the Great Barrier Reef and it is usually freely available. Many island resorts have their own experienced dive leaders and many of them will give instruction in scuba diving and snorkelling techniques. Charter boat captains are also familiar with the reef, know the good dive spots and know the dangers.

Preparing to dive

Careful preparation is vital to diving, and the chief requirement is to be medically fit. Many dive leaders, whether at resorts, on charter boats or with dive tours, insist on evidence of a diving orientated medical examination carried out within the past twelve months before taking that person on a diving excursion.

While the skills for snorkelling are minimal, scuba diving is a highly technical pastime, and it does require initial training in the use of scuba gear. At all resorts and on most charter boats, evidence of having qualified from an accepted scuba course must be shown, or alternately, a basic training course can be undertaken over several days while holidaying on some of the islands.

Scuba gear and safety

After training, equipment is the next priority. Travelling with scuba equipment is often a bother and most resorts and other dive operators carry a range of equipment for hire provided that acceptable diving qualifications are held by the hirer. Awkward tanks and weight belts especially are readily available for hire.

Before leaving home, it is a good idea to check all personal gear, and have the regulator and any other gauges serviced. The Standards Association of Australia covers the manufacture, testing and filling of steel and aluminium cylinders, and these standards are enforced by the Department of Occupational Safety in Queensland.

All diving cylinders must be hydrostatically tested by a Standards Association approved testing station every year, and filling stations generally will not fill a cylinder which is out of test.

Rules of the reef

Knowledge of local rules is extremely important. Throughout Australia the recognised diving flag is the international flag code A, a blue and white swallow-tailed burgee. The size of the diving flag should be a minimum of one metre by one metre so that it can be easily seen. The flag should always be flown when divers or snorkellers are in the water and under local boating regulations this signifies 'I have a diver below – keep well clear at low speed'.

Australia is in the enviable position of possessing the largest marine park in the world. The Great Barrier Reef Marine Park, covering the whole of the reef, has a number of rules that must be adhered to. Local divers will undoubtedly know the local rules but, in some instances, prior permits are required for certain activities or areas. Before camping on one of the islands, ownership should be ascertained. If the island is a private holding, permission of the owner is required. If the island is

crown land, it may be reserved for special purposes such as Aboriginal Reserves or National Parks and consequently there may be permit requirements.

Finally, Australia has a 'Historic Shipwrecks Act' that prohibits diving on any declared historic wreck in Australian waters. Many shipwrecks have occurred along the Great Barrier Reef but only a handful of these have been proclaimed historic. Some of these can be dived but only after a permit has been obtained. Ships from many countries, such as Spain, Portugal, Britain and Holland, have been lost here.

This is not a comprehensive review of the laws and rules relating to diving and associated activities; it must be emphasised that local knowledge can increase awareness of the limitations and restrictions that are placed on all users of the Great Barrier Reef. But diving on the reef is still remarkably easy and must rate as one of the greatest possible wilderness adventures.☐

◁ Once underwater, a new world opens up to the scuba diver or the snorkeller. There are endless coral gardens to be explored, thousands of species of plants and animals to be found and photographed. Caves, canyons and vertical drop-offs are there to be investigated, above, each with its own photogenic inhabitants.

'One can hover like a bird above the kaleidoscopic pastures of the reef. Diving here is a rich and rewarding adventure ... and a very private one.'

Conserving for the future: scientific research

An ecological puzzle

Coral reefs are among the world's most diverse and complex ecosystems. Our scientific understanding of how they work is far from satisfactory and is well behind our understanding of all other ecosystems, except perhaps those in Antarctica. This is in part because many universities and other centres of learning are concentrated in the temperate regions of the northern hemisphere, well away from coral reefs.

Early navigators in the Pacific, while surveying in the reef, often reported on the natural history of the region. Many naturalists visited the reef on survey vessels: J. Beete Jukes, who sailed with Captain F. P. Blackwood on HMS *Fly* in 1843, was the first scientific investigator of the Great Barrier Reef. His work was primarily geological and provided evidence for Darwin's theories. T. H. Huxley and J. MacGillivray sailed on HMS *Rattlesnake* in 1852 and were more involved with the reef's fascinating natural history. Towards the end of the 19th century Saville Kent published several reports, at the request of the Queensland Government, on the marine resources and fisheries of north Queensland. Among these was his classical, superbly illustrated volume entitled *The Great Barrier Reef*, published in 1893.

Established research

In 1922, the formation of a Great Barrier Reef Committee within the Queensland branch of the Royal Geographical Society of Australia marked the beginning of concerted research into the reef. Disagreements with the Royal Geographical Society later led to the committee's separation from its parent body. Recently, the Great Barrier Reef Committee has been reconstituted, and it is now known as the Australian Coral Reef Society.

One of the first projects undertaken by the original committee was the drilling in 1926 of a 183-metre bore-hole in Michaelmas Cay, near Cairns, under the supervision of Charles Hedley. A second, 223-metre bore was later drilled at Heron Island in 1937, but neither of these provided information to satisfy the geological questions about subsidence and the growth of coral reefs.

In 1928, the Great Barrier Reef Committee collaborated with the Royal Society of London to co-ordinate the first major biological expedition to the reef. For over 13 months, a team of 23 scientists, led by Sir Maurice Yonge, occupied a small field laboratory on Low Isles, off Port Douglas. The results of their studies, published over several decades by the British Museum of Natural History, are still being used today, although the buildings have long since disappeared.

Since then, four island research stations have been established to support scientific research into coral reefs. Three of these are operated by universities: on Heron Island by Queensland University, on One Tree Island by Sydney University and on Orpheus Island by James Cook University. The fourth is operated by the Australian Museum at Lizard Island in the northern region of the Great Barrier Reef.

In 1972 the Federal Government established a large research centre located 50 kilometres south of Townsville: the Australian Institute of Marine Science (AIMS). The research programs of the Institute are directed towards understanding the key environmental and ecosystem processes of the Great Barrier Reef region. In particular, the focus is on five main areas: the mangrove systems of northern Australia, the near-shore coastal environment within the reef lagoon, the oceanography of the continental shelf of the region, and two programs that attempt to understand and describe coral reef systems.

One of these major programs is designed to gain an understanding of the metabolic process leading to the development, growth and maintenance of coral reefs. The other program covers studies of the nature and extent of the distribution of corals and the associated plants and animals of the reef.

Researchers in Australian universities – notably James Cook University of North Queensland in Townsville and the universities of Sydney and Brisbane – and from overseas institutions, make major contributions to our knowledge of the reef ecosystem. The island research stations and AIMS provide the basic facilities utilised by these researchers. Facilities are now much better on the reef, although there is still a need in the far north. Assistance for all but AIMS is tenuous, however, with no permanent Commonwealth support.

The techniques and equipment used to study the reef are as diverse as the reef itself. In the early days much work was done by remote methods – dredges, nets, bottom grabs and explosive. A major boost was given to marine studies, following World War II, with the manufacture of self-contained underwater breathing apparatus (scuba), which permitted scientists to directly observe the life and behaviour of the reef organisms.

At one end of the scale, biologists are unravelling the mysteries of physiological processes using electron microscopes to 'see' into algal cells, while geologists are using x-ray diffractometers and radiocarbon dating to determine growth rates of corals and clams, which can then be used to date the reef structure. At the other end of the spectrum are the high technology remote sensing devices aboard earth satellites, which can show structures of whole reefs, indicate water-mass movements and determine large-scale patterns of distribution of corals and algae in shallow water.

Direct underwater observation by diving scientists, however, has been the basis of modern reef discoveries. Researchers often spend many hours a day underwater. Records are kept on underwater slates of perspex or polystyrene, and supplemented by underwater photographs. These long-term projects have provided insights into such phenomena as sex reversal in reef fishes, territories and home ranges, and the mass spawning of corals on just one or two nights a year.

The advent of small personal computers is also expanding research. Many studies now generate such vast data banks that analyses can only be performed by computers. Another approach being used at the Lizard Island research station is to take photographs of experimental ascidian colonies from fixed distances, develop and enlarge the photographs by a set amount, then place these photographs directly on a digitiser connected to a computer from which immediate measurements of area, change in area and growth rates of the colony can be obtained. Microprocessors and data loggers are also becoming widely used for continuously monitoring the reef, especially locations that are not safe for humans, such as the reef front during a cyclone.

Where does the water go?

One of the fundamental questions essential to an understanding of many reef processes is that of water movements within the reef province. At what rate is water exchanged between the Great Barrier Reef and the Coral Sea and through Torres Strait? What are the effects of trade or monsoon winds on surface water movements? And where do the deeper waters go? Answers to these questions are important for shipping, and for predicting the progress of pollutants, or of the larvae of reef organisms.

At a more restricted scale there are important questions to be answered to describe the patterns of wakes and eddies that occur in the lee of reefs and islands. Recent work shows that these water bodies are important for maintaining or returning the larvae of reef organisms to their parent reef system.

At the microscopic level we need to know how water passes over a reef and between the actual branches of the corals to carry nutrients and remove waste products from the system.

Another major field of interest is that of the population dynamics of reef organisms. What are the geographical limits of a local population? What are the growth rates of the individuals? What is the carrying capacity of the environment? What impact do man's activities – such as increasing nutrient levels – have on the growth of local populations? When and where does spawning take place? If a local population is overfished or destroyed by a cyclone how long will it take the population to recover, and where will the new population come from? What factors control the populations of crown-of-thorns starfish? These problems are of paramount importance if the living reef is to be managed properly and if the enormous diversity of species is to be retained.

The reef's resources

The Great Barrier Reef region is protected from extensive resource development by the Great Barrier Reef Marine Park Act of 1975, the establishment of the Great Barrier Reef Marine Park, and the 1981 inscription of the Great Barrier Reef on the World Heritage List. The resources that can be exploited in the Park are renewable, 'living' resources and the water itself. The variety of living resources is probably far greater in a tropical reef system than in any other marine habitat.
Since the early 20th century – when bêche-de-mer, trochus shells and turtles were exploited commercially – the reef's principal 'living' resource has been food: fishes and prawns from wild stock. In more recent years the Moreton Bay 'bug' has also been fished. A small pearl oyster industry has existed for many years in the far northern Great Barrier Reef and in Torres Strait.

Additionally, there have been small enterprises based on hard coral and shell collecting for the tourist trade, and the trochus shell industry was re-established in the early 1980s on reefs near Mackay and the Whitsunday Islands.

However, in none of these – except the pearl oyster industry – have farming techniques been introduced to guarantee continuity of supply. Until now, the demand for fishes has never exceeded the supply, and therefore little attention has been given to mariculture: farming of the sea. On the Great Barrier Reef, the cultivation of prawns both for stock replenishment and for production to commercial size, is now a priority.

Salt, water and alternative food

Small industries have been established for the recovery of salt from marine waters and, eventually, the recovery of fresh water from sea water may be one of the most important resources in dry, tropical areas.

The reef is also proving to be a rich source of alternative food products and species from which chemicals, biochemicals or polymers can be produced. Marine polymers such as agar, carrageenan and alginates – mainly from seaweeds – are used as gel stabilisers in ice-cream, for the fining of wines, and in cake and pie constituents.

A number of toxic and venomous species of plants and animals occur in the reef region, including various cone shellfish, Conidae; the blue-ringed octopus, *Hapelochlaena maculosa*; the stonefish, *Synanceja trachynis*; the box jellyfish or sea wasp, *Chironex fleckeri*, and the crown-of-thorns starfish, *Acanthaster planci*. The presence of these species has encouraged research into their toxins to

test suitability for medical and veterinary use. Bacteria, algae, sponges, hard and soft corals, sea anemones, molluscs and fishes were investigated. Scientists established that the active principle of the blue-ringed octopus's toxin is tetrodotoxin, which is also found in the pufferfish. They also discovered that the infections and ulcerations that follow coral scratches were almost always caused by three closely related species of marine bacteria, which were resistant to penicillin, ampicillin and carbenicillin – the antibiotics often recommended first – but were sensitive to tetracyclin and to erythromycin.

Early adventurers

For many thousands of years, human impact on the Great Barrier Reef was probably restricted to the immediate requirements of a relatively sparse coastal population who did not develop a major seagoing tradition. It was settlement of the Australian

mainland by another wave of immigrants about 200 years ago that heralded the beginning of more intensive and widespread use of the natural resources of north Queensland and the reef.

Early commercial users of the reef relied upon coastal shipping and small boats. They sought bêche-de-mer, or trepang, turtle shell and meat, oil from dugongs, oysters, trochus shells and fishes for local consumption. Few areas of the reef were not explored by these early adventurers. Modern motor vessels with freezers, and trawlers have increased the range of both commercial and amateur operations, and proposals have been put forward in other areas, such as tourism and mineral exploration and extraction.

With the growing use of the reef and the slow accumulation of knowledge of some of the physical and biological characteristics of the area has come the realisation that the Great Barrier Reef is not

only an area of national significance; it is also the largest system of coral and its associated life in the world. It is a part of the world's heritage.

The question is how, in the face of continually increasing pressures and demands on its resources, do we ensure that this area remains in perpetuity for inspiration, for enjoyment and recreation, and also as a source of livelihood for those who depend more directly on its natural resources? How are decisions to be made on uses that are compatible with its conservation; how are reference areas to be established so that changes due to human activity can be detected above the seasonal and other cyclic changes that may occur naturally, and how are conflicts between potential users to be avoided?

Environmental protection

In the late 1960s and early 1970s there was growing environmental concern in Australia and an

△ *A battery-operated 'wet' submarine allows diving scientists to carry extra tanks or heavy equipment to underwater work sites, or to travel long distances for underwater surveys or to follow large fishes, such as sharks. The submarine is a retreat on occasions when sharks under observation become a little too inquisitive.*

'The biological and geological complexity of the Great Barrier Reef make it the richest marine habitat on earth.'

increasing awareness that the Great Barrier Reef needed protection if its wonderful riches were to be retained. There was an outcry when drilling for oil was to be started on the reef. A great many Australians considered that the area should be totally protected from mining and other development to preserve it in as natural a state as possible. There were, however, established users: a number of people make their living from the area, and it was also considered possible that reserves of oil or other scarce mineral resources may have been present. Some sections of the community thought that serious consideration should have been given to the costs and benefits of extracting those resources.

While a great deal can be achieved by individuals and concerned groups acting to protect areas in which there is an obvious or immediate threat, the conservation and protection of an area as large as the Great Barrier Reef requires a firm basis in the existing framework of government.

The Marine Park Act

Early disputes between the State and Commonwealth governments over control of the sea and seabed off Australia hampered the development of an integrated approach to conservation of the Great Barrier Reef. In 1975, the Great Barrier Reef Marine Park Authority was formed under an Act of the Australian Parliament, which provided for the protection of the area while recognising the need to accommodate reasonable use. (Before 1975, the Queensland Government had also recognised the need for conservation, and had declared the Heron and Wistari Reefs and the Green Island Reef as Marine Parks.) Under the 1975 Federal legislation the one use not permitted is mining for minerals, including oil, except for approved research.

The Great Barrier Reef Marine Park Act provides for extensive public participation. The Act is Commonwealth legislation, but because it has profound implications for the State of Queensland, provision is made for co-ordination between State and Commonwealth interests. One of the three members of the Great Barrier Reef Marine Park Authority is nominated by the Queensland Government. The Authority is responsible to a Commonwealth Minister, who is the convener of a ministerial council made up of two Queensland and two Commonwealth Ministers, intended to co-ordinate the policies of the two governments on Great Barrier Reef matters. Additional advice to the Federal Minister and the Authority comes from a large consultative committee, which receives advice and requests from various government authorities, conservation organisations, tourist, commercial and recreational fishing, and other interest groups.

The major functions of the Authority and its staff are the identification and delineation of areas that are to be included in the Marine Park and the preparation and monitoring of zoning plans.

Because the Act applies only to the waters and seabed of the region, with all islands other than those used for defence or navigational purposes under the control of the Queensland Government, co-ordination of the zoning plans with existing controls on the islands is important. Although the Great Barrier Reef Marine Park Act provides the legislative basis for the care and development of the area to which it applies, it can only function effectively with support from an informed and sympathetic public. Three opportunities are provided for public comment between the declaration of the outer boundaries of a section of the Park and the implementation of a zoning plan.

Some people consider that the term Marine Park for the whole region is a misnomer, as commercial exploitation of natural resources is allowed in extensive areas within the region, although it is controlled by the zoning plan and management practices. They claim that the entire region should be subject to the same degree of protection found in major national parks, with smaller areas identified for commercial and other potentially damaging uses. Others believe that the protection of particularly sensitive areas by zoning and management controls to accommodate a variety of uses will ensure the conservation of the entire area generally accepted as the Great Barrier Reef. The zoning process at present identifies areas within a section in which no extractive or potentially damaging activities are permitted. Areas adjacent to particularly sensitive localities or features may be set aside as buffer zones, providing broader scale protection by progressively excluding activities that may damage the reef and its animals and plants, or by regulating the intensity of those activities.

A long-term reference area

In contrast to terrestrial ecosystems, in which there may be comparatively little import of nutrients and energy, other than those in water and from sunlight, water movement and current systems are extremely important in the maintenance of the reef. We still do not know how large an area of the reef has to be maintained in an undisturbed state to serve as a long-term reference area.

Three main areas are of primary importance: research, to provide the information necessary for good decisions; monitoring, to assess the impact of those decisions; and education, to provide information to the community and to create a climate in which conservation practices are accepted by the reef's users.

The future of the reef

The biological and geological complexity of the Great Barrier Reef make it the richest marine habitat on earth, and it increases in relative value as other areas of coral reef come under stress, often from communities whose needs for the very basics

of life demand reef use. The largest remaining herds of the gentle dugong are in reef waters, the world's greatest mass breeding of turtles occurs on Raine Island and breeding sites of many sea birds are situated the length and breadth of the reef.

However, the living reef can be – and has been – damaged. Its dugongs are easily killed accidentally in fishermen's nets. Its turtle populations can be reduced by the careless use of their breeding islands. Many of the bird populations cannot tolerate human interference at nesting time, and eggs and nestlings may be destroyed by rats introduced with human habitation. The beautifully adapted island vegetation can be transformed by human introductions, deliberate and accidental.

Since the formation of the Great Barrier Reef Marine Park Authority a new perspective of the reef has been formed, much of which bears on how it is to be protected. Whereas the reef was previously regarded as a relatively unchanging system, with stable populations of most species from year to year, it is now known to be highly dynamic. A species that is abundant one year may have a poor recruitment the next year; populations may become extinct on one patch of coral or on a complete reef, and follow this with a number of successful years.

The rise and fall in the numbers of crown-of-thorns starfish were startling because they made severe inroads on the corals on which they feed: the living surface of the reef. But skeletal pieces in lagoon sands have established that even the coral-eating starfish has had population booms before. And the fluctuations noted in other reef species suggest that this behaviour is perhaps not abnormal.

Inshore reefs differ from those near the outer barrier, and researchers have documented changes in the abundance and food sources of fish communities across the reef. Many of the reef's inhabitants produce floating eggs or larvae, some of which float for two to three weeks before settling. The strong currents of the reef may move fish larvae hundreds of kilometres from their parent reef, leaving them little possibility of resettling on it. Oceanographers have discovered that long period waves may generate alternately reversing currents of about 500 kilometres along the southern reef area. These two facts, from different disciplines, have an obvious conservation message – the protection of a reef is pointless if surrounding areas are damaged.

In geologists' terms the reef is young – only about two million years old – and the last low-sea-level period, which lasted 100 000 years, stripped off up to 15 metres of reef surface. The present period of reef growth, building on older reef platforms, has already lasted for 8000 years, but the future may hold another erosional period. In that event people may again be able to walk to the outer edge of the reef, as the early Aboriginal Australians did long ago. For the forseeable future, however, the reef in its present state is in our hands. □

Islands and resorts: making a choice

Many of the Great Barrier Reef's islands and the mainland coastal towns in the area have excellent tourist facilities and are easily accessible; other islands are suitable only for day trippers and campers. Whatever your choice, make a visit and experience at first hand the beauty and diversity of the reef's flora and fauna.

Above ground, you can take a walk through lush green rainforests, hike up a small mountain, see the sea bird or turtle rookeries where breeding takes place every year, or picnic on a secluded beach in a protected cove (all the resorts with full facilities will pack a picnic lunch for you). And at low tide you can stroll over exposed corals where miniature communities live happily in rock pools.

Your first sight of an exposed coral reef may not live up to expectations; corals that are not regularly immersed in the sea lose their brilliance and colour. Only on a coral cay will a reef walk reveal their true splendour.

Tides have a big range – six metres or more – in reef regions, so take note of the tide times advised by the resorts. Always wear strong-soled shoes, as coral can inflict nasty scratches and poisonous stonefish may lie in shallow pools and crevices. As you're walking, avoid breaking fragile forms of coral or turning over shells; most of the islands are National Parks and all living creatures are protected.

Glass-bottomed boats and semi-submersibles will reveal more of the magical underwater scene of brilliant colours and fascinating shapes. Underwater observatories and aquariums also offer close-up views. And if you want to go 'down under', you can learn to snorkel or scuba dive at the island schools. Only then will you enter the strange world of coral gardens, brightly coloured fishes – some tiny and elusive, some aggressive and cheeky – and meadows of sea grass grazed by shy dugongs. Look closely at a coral boulder and see the bizarre spirals of Christmas tree worms and the holes made by boring sponges. And marvel at the tiny coral polyp, more like a plant than an animal, which builds the reef's framework.

To learn to dive properly – and safely – be prepared to spend at least five days on an accredited course (and don't forget to take a recent medical certificate of fitness with you). And also be prepared to wait out unfavourable weather conditions. If you're not on a coral cay on the Reef itself, diving trips from the resorts will be cancelled on windy days. All water sports, in fact, are subject to tide and weather conditions.

Every section of the Reef has much to offer, but no matter which area you choose to visit, never forget that you are entering the tropics. Light, natural fibre clothing is the best choice, and always take care, especially on your first day, to avoid sunburn. Wear a hat and a protective sun cream . . . and enjoy your holiday.

▽ *On a Barrier Reef holiday you can fill every minute of the day with a diverse range of activities . . . or simply soak up the spectacular surroundings.*

Brampton Island

Southern Reef islands

There are three islands in the Capricornia section of the Great Barrier Reef Marine Park that have resort facilities: Great Keppel, Heron and Lady Elliot. One other island, Lady Musgrave, is accessible to day trippers and campers. All campers must have permits from the Queensland National Parks and Wildlife Service.

Two of the three resort islands are on the Reef itself, making the southern section ideal for direct diving, without the need for boat trips to the Outer Reef. Their distance from the mainland also ensures less rainfall.

Temperatures in the region are mild to warm, with an average of 22°C in winter and 28°C in summer. Summer humidity can be high; two-thirds of the annual rainfall occurs between October and May, with January–March the wettest period.

Bundaberg (372 km N of Brisbane; daily flights) is the southern gateway to the Reef with access to Lady Elliot Island and day trips to Lady Musgrave Island. This is the only access point that can provide reef trips for day visitors from the Gold Coast, Brisbane and the Sunshine Coast.

Gladstone (558 km N of Brisbane; daily flights) is the access point for Heron Island, either by helicopter or by launch. Day trips to coral cays, such as the 1½-hour catamaran trip to Mast Head Island, and charter fishing trips are also available.

Rockhampton (641 km N of Brisbane; daily flights) is an access point for Great Keppel Island by air.

Yeppoon (689 km N of Brisbane; daily flights to Rockhampton then bus to Yeppoon) has a luxury resort and is the access point for Great Keppel Island by charter boat from Rosslyn Bay. Day cruises in the Keppel group are also available from the modern boat harbour.

Great Keppel Island

This 1454-hectare continental island in the Keppel group is a flora and fauna sanctuary, with a fringing reef and 28 kilometres of sandy beaches. It can be reached by air from Rockhampton daily (20 minutes); by boat from Rosslyn Bay daily (50 minutes). Day trips are available.

Accommodation: 160 self-contained beachfront, garden or family units, with balcony, ceiling fan, refrigerator, tea and coffee making facilities. Resort facilities include guest laundry, public telephones, shop, hairdressing salon, disco, 6-hole golf course, 3 day/night tennis courts, 2 squash courts, 3 swimming pools, spa, outdoor fitness circuit.
Dress: Very casual by day; smart casual for evening (no thongs).
Atmosphere: Lively and organised; for the young.
Children's facilities: Special club for 3–13-year-olds during gazetted school holidays. Special children's

dinner (5.30 pm–6 pm) for children over three, with free child-minding service from 5.30 pm to 8.30 pm. Wading pool. Playground. Hire chairs available in restaurant. Strollers, baby baths, nappy buckets and infant carryback packs available. Baby-sitting at normal rates.
Reef-related activities: Scuba diving. Snorkelling trips to Middle Island. Around-island cruises. Charter fishing trips. Coral viewing by glass-bottom boat. Special boat charters. Daily helicopter Reef trips. Visits to Middle Island underwater observatory.
Other activities: Windsurfing, bushwalking, catamarans, beach cricket, golf, tennis, archery, squash, swimming, netball, softball, volleyball, paddle skis, aqua bikes, para-sailing, fishing, outboard dinghies, aerobics, boom-netting, badminton, table tennis, darts, water-skiing, basketball, horse riding, racquetball, soccer, touch football, underwater hockey, water tobogganing, inland water cruises,

Heron Island; Wistari Reef

△ *Heron Island and Wistari Reef are among the best known reefs in the Great Barrier Reef region. Wistari has a completely enclosed lagoon with a mosaic of patch reefs. Heron's lagoon is shallower, especially around the cay. The artificial boat channel cut into the reef adjacent to the cay can be clearly seen. The channel has accelerated the ebb currents draining the reef flat near the island, resulting in the removal of sediment and serious erosion problems around the resort on the far end of the cay.*

jogging, pinball machines, trips to restored 19th century homestead.
Tariff: All inclusive (except liquor, fuel-powered sporting equipment, charters): $117–$139 per person twin share per day.
Contact: Bookings through Australian Airlines.

Heron Island

A true coral cay in which 12 of the 17 hectares are a National Park, Heron has a research station run by the University of Queensland. The powdered coral beaches are white, and the clear waters and platform reefs support some of the best fish life and living coral anywhere in the world. From October to March, green and loggerhead turtles lay their eggs on the beaches. All marine life is protected, beach fishing is not allowed, spear-fishing is forbidden. Camping is not permitted on the island. Heron Island is reached by launch (2 hours), helicopter charter service (30 minutes), or charter boats, all from Gladstone. Day trips are available.

Accommodation: 95 rooms, from self-contained, air-conditioned suites with patios, to budget-priced lodges with share facilities. Resort facilities include public telephones, a TV room, boutique/general store, tennis court, swimming pool.
Dress: Casual by day; smart casual by night.
Atmosphere: Intimate and relaxing.
Children's facilities: Children not catered for.
Reef-related activities: Diving is the principal activity, with a professional diving course available; best months for diving are October, November, December; dive boats depart twice daily. Fish and coral viewing in a semi-submersible submarine. Snorkelling. Daily guided reef walks. Reef videos. Cruises to other islands. Charter boats for ½ and 1-day fishing trips.
Other activities: Birdwatching, turtle viewing, table tennis, billiards.
Tariff: All inclusive (except liquor, fuel-powered sporting equipment, charters): $90–$160 per person twin share per day.
Contact: (07) 268 8224.

Lady Elliot Island

At the southern extremity of the GBR Marine Park, Lady Elliot Island is a 42-hectare coral cay totally surrounded by fringing reef, with clear, calm water and white coral beaches. The reefs are rich with marine life, including manta rays, turtles and reef sharks, much to the delight of divers, and the island is one of the most significant bird rookeries off the Australian coast (October to April). Lady Elliot can be reached by air from Bundaberg daily (20 minutes).

Accommodation: Beachside cabins with private

Lady Elliot Island

Great Keppel Island

White-capped noddy tern

△ △ *While Great Keppell is a continental island with vast stretches of sandy beach, Lady Elliot, in the Bunker group, is a true coral cay, a natural formation caused by the accumulation of sediments derived from the carbonate-secreting plants and animals of the reef.*

△ ▷ *Lady Musgrave is another coral cay and shows typical reef zonation: outer seaward slope beyond the white breaker zone, algal-dominated outer reef flat, inner reef flat terminating on the lagoon side, shallow sand flat and the lagoon itself, containing discrete patch reefs. The island has no resort facilities but offers an abundance of birdlife and good reef walking and snorkelling.*

Lady Musgrave Island

Lady Musgrave Reef

facilities; safari tents for one-four people, with beds; cabins without facilities. There is a shop, but no telephone, TV or radios.

Dress: Casual.

Atmosphere: Casual and relaxed; individuals, families and groups welcome.

Children's facilities: Cots available.

Reef-related activities: Good diving – best months October, November, December; professional diving instructors; shore, boat and night dives; underwater diving trail. Snorkelling. Glass-bottom boat. Guided daily reef walks. Boat fishing trips. Fish feeding.

Other activities: Walking tracks, volleyball, board games, jogging, coral pool swimming.

Tariff: All inclusive (except liquor, equipment hire, charters): $75–$100 per person twin share per day.

Contact; (008) 07 2200 (toll-free).

The Cumberland and Whitsunday Islands

Most of the islands in the central section of the Great Barrier Reef Marine Park are uninhabited, densely forested National Parks. There are eight islands with resort facilities: Brampton, Daydream, Hamilton, Hayman, Hook, Lindeman, Long and South Molle. Some islands, without resorts, are popular with day visitors: Shute, Tancred and Repair. Camping holidays (permits required) are also available on other islands, with basic camping facilities provided by the Queensland National Parks and Wildlife Service: Gloucester, Saddleback, Armit (access from Dingo Beach); Whitsunday, North Molle, Henning, Shute, Thomas (access from Shute Harbour); Goldsmith,

South Repulse, Rabbit and Outer Newry (access from Mackay). Many of the smaller islands have shallow bays offering good anchorage.

The Whitsunday Passage is considered one of the safest cruising grounds in the world. The region is tropical, with temperatures which vary only slightly over the year. From April to October (the cruising season) daytime temperatures range from 20°C–24°C, with 14°C–18°C at night. During the hotter months of November to March, the temperature climbs and tropical showers prevail; temperatures range from 24°C–30°C during the day, and 18°C–26°C at night. Throughout the year, water temperature remains at a constant 20-22 degrees.

Rainfall around the Whitsundays and Cumberlands is substantial enough to sustain luxuriant vegetation on the islands. The period from

Heron Reef

△ *The reef off Heron Island is rich in marine life and can be enjoyed both by the scuba diver and by viewing from the resort's semi-submersible.*

▷ △ *The Whitsunday Passage, top, offers safe boating for tourist craft and private boats which wend their way among the 74 islands in the area.*

Whitsunday Passage

Brampton Island

December to February is the wettest, though the offshore resorts are generally drier and sunnier than the mainland coast.

Because of the great number of islands in the Whitsunday Passage, the water channels at great speed and churns up sediment; there are strong tidal rips all year round and the water is often murky, offering poor visibility for near-shore diving. All the Whitsunday resorts offer diving trips to the Outer Reef.

Mackay (1019 km N of Brisbane, 150 km S of Airlie Beach; daily flights) is the access point for Brampton Island, as well as for charter boats to other islands. Launches based at Port Mackay operate day trips through the Passage and longer trips to outer reefs. There are over 30 beaches in the Mackay area, and rainforested mainland National Parks.

Proserpine (1107 km N of Brisbane; daily flights) is the access point for helicopters direct to Daydream, Hamilton, Lindeman and South Molle Islands, and for sea-plane to Hayman Island. Proserpine is also the pickup point for regular coach services to Shute Harbour and Airlie.

Shute Harbour (1178 km N of Brisbane, 36 km E of Proserpine; daily flights to Proserpine, then bus) is the access point for all the Whitsunday island resorts. A one-time fishermen's retreat, it is now a bustling centre for buses, cruising craft and charter boats. Several companies specialise in chartering fully provisioned small boats for self-sail holidays. Day cruises and amphibian flights, scheduled according to the tides, leave Shute Harbour every day. Helicopter flights operate to a helipad on the Outer Reef (some 70 km from the coast). Water taxis can be hired from

Shute Harbour to any Whitsunday island location. A glass-bottom boat operates over the reefs fringing the small islands in Shute Harbour.

Shute Harbour also has an airstrip for scenic flights over the Whitsundays and trips to the Reef. There are regular air services between Mackay, Townsville and Cairns.

Airlie (26 km E of Proserpine) has resorts and caravan parks to cater for visitors planning trips to the islands as well as those staying in the area. Cruises and fishing boats also operate from Airlie, the main resort town on the Whitsunday Coast. Although most island cruises operate from Shute Harbour, there are several sailing and diving trips which set out daily from Airlie Beach. Dive courses of all kinds are available. Packaged island-hopping holidays include resorts at Airlie.

Daydream (West Molle) Island

Shute Harbour

Airlie

△ *West Molle Island, popularly called Daydream, is typical of the Whitsunday islands. Though small, away from the resort area it still shows the rough, hilly terrain indicative of the peaks of a mountain range that was flooded by rising sea levels about 8000 years ago.*

◁ *Brampton Island, in the Cumberland group, is joined by a coral reef to undeveloped Carlisle Island; the narrow channel can be crossed on foot at low tide.*

▷ *Coastal ranges plunge abruptly into the waters of the Whitsunday Passage; huddled around the bays are the busy tourist towns of Shute Harbour, top, and Airlie, backed by the densely rainforested Conway National Park. All activity in the area is centred on the towns, as cruising yachts, launches and water taxis head for holiday resorts and uninhabited national park islands which rise from the waters of the continental shelf, sheltered by outer coral formations of the Great Barrier Reef.*

Brampton Island

This continental island of 78 hectares is a National Park, with a resort at Sandy Point. Part of the Cumberlands group, Brampton has seven sandy beaches, a 219-metre peak and extensive wildlife, including turtles and birds. Camping is not permitted. The island is reached by air (20 minutes) or catamaran (45 minutes), both from Mackay. Day trips are available.

Accommodation: 120 self-contained units, with air-conditioning, refrigerator, radio, tea and coffee making facilities, iron and ironing board. Resort facilities include a restaurant-entertainment complex, four bars, coffee shop, gift shop, gymnasium, games room, freshwater and saltwater pools, 3 tennis courts, 5-hole golf course, spa, sauna, public telephones and guest laundry.
Dress: Neat and casual; more dressy for dinner.
Atmosphere: Secluded and informal; high incidence of honeymooners.
Children's facilities: Special dinner sitting. Activities program in school holidays. High chairs available in restaurant. Baby-sitting at normal rates.
Reef-related activities: Coral viewing by glass-bottom boat. Reef cruises and flights. Whitsunday cruises. Fishing trips. Diving trips. There is a 6-metre difference between low and high tides; snorkelling is better at low tide; catamarans and sailboards cannot go out until sand bars are covered; tides noted in daily newsletter. Walks at low tide to Carlisle Island.
Other activities: Fishing, catamarans, water trikes, archery, TV (video) lounge, beach volleyball, carpet bowls, tennis, golf, surf skis, windsurfing, water-skiing, water tobogganing, pools and billiards, bushwalking (7 km trail around island), aerobics, table tennis, basketball, cricket, jogging, paddle skis, safe beach swimming.
Tariff: All inclusive (except liquor, fuel-powered sporting equipment, charters): $120–$150 per person twin share per day.
Contact: Bookings through Australian Airlines.

▷ △ *All the resorts in the Whitsunday islands provide safe swimming beaches and a range of water sports and activities. The calm waters of the Passage are ideal for catamaran sailing and canoeing.*

▷ *A readily accessible way to come face to face with the sheer beauty of a reef is with a mask and a snorkel. Drifting in the clear, shallow water of a lagoon reveals the colour and contrast of coral marine life.*

Daydream Island

Norman Reef

Daydream Island

Passage Peak, Hamilton Island

Daydream (West Molle) Island

Daydream – at 11 hectares, the smallest of the settled islands in the area – is a privately owned, densely forested continental island with tropical rainforests and quiet coral sand beaches. Camping is not permitted. It is reached by ferry from Shute Harbour several times daily (20 minutes); by water taxi from Hamilton Island (40 minutes); by helicopter from Proserpine (5 minutes). Day trips are available.

Accommodation: 96 self-contained units, with air conditioning, colour TV, radio, refrigerator, tea and coffee making facilities, direct-dial telephone, iron and ironing board. Resort facilities include saltwater and freshwater swimming pools, tennis court, spa and sauna, gift shop, guest laundry, three bars, laundry and dry cleaning service.
Dress: Casual; smart casual at night.
Atmosphere: Friendly and fun; guests mostly under 30.
Children's facilities: Special activities can be arranged; also early dining. Wading pool. Baby-sitting at normal rates.
Reef-related activities: Snorkelling. Scuba diving; full dive facilities. Cruises to nearby resorts, mainland, uninhabited islands. Glass-bottom boat for coral viewing (also submarine and float plane). Seaplane and helicopter flights and launch and catamaran trips to Reef for reef walking and coral viewing. Reef trips for divers and snorkellers. Underwater observatory. Fishing trips. Boat charters.
Other activities: Tennis, bushwalking, catamarans, windsurfing, canoes, paddle skis, swimming, pool tables, video machines, volleyball, table tennis, safe beach swimming (shoes recommended), dinghies, para-sailing, water-skiing, boom-netting, mini speed boats, badminton, billiards, aqua paddle cat.
Tariff: All inclusive (except liquor, fuel-powered sporting equipment, charters): $99–$120 per person twin share per day.
Contact: (008) 07 5040 (toll-free).

◁ △ *No matter the time of day, there is always activity around the Whitsunday islands. Away from the narrow shipping channel, the quiet waters are a playground for holiday-makers, who can skim along on a sled or tube ride, soar above the peaks while para-sailing, or simply wait in a boat moored offshore for the start of another day.*

Daydream Island

Hamilton Island

This 607-hectare continental island with fringing reef has been substantially developed but includes an 80-hectare wildlife park and a dolphin pool. There are direct flights from Melbourne, Sydney, Brisbane, Cairns, Rockhampton and Ayers Rock to the island's jet airstrip, and connections with international flights. Hamilton can also be reached by boat from Shute Harbour (35 minutes); by charter boat from Mackay; by helicopter from Proserpine (20 minutes). Day trips are available.

Accommodation: 400 self-contained bures, lodge units and highrise apartments with air conditioning, balcony, tea and coffee making facilities, refrigerator, mini-bar, TV, radio, telephone, iron and ironing board; some specially designed rooms for the handicapped. Resort facilities at Catseye Beach include 6 tennis courts, 2 squash courts, 6 freshwater swimming pools, spa, sauna, gymnasium, restaurants, bars, games room with video games, pinball machines, table tennis and board games, and a shopping centre. The harbourside village has a 200-berth marina, restaurants, shops and bars.
Dress: Smart casual to dressy.
Atmosphere: Relaxed, upmarket; popular with yachtsmen.
Children's facilities: Children's club.
Reef-related activities: Snorkelling trips. Boat trips to Reef. Boat trips to Dent Island coral art studio. Sailing trips. Twilight canoe cruises. Helicopter flights to floating pontoon on Reef for coral viewing by submarine, snorkelling or scuba diving. Diving instructions and trip to Reef. Extended cruises (5-day, 7-day).
Other activities: Jet skis, catamarans, para-sailing, water-skiing, windsurfing, surf skis, outrigger canoes, water volleyball, aerobics, tennis, squash, bushwalking, dinghy hire, billiards, swimming, paddle boards.
Tariff: Accommodation only: from $175 (per room; 1 or 2 people) to $1375 (penthouse suite) per day.
Contact: (079) 46 9144. (008) 07 5110 (toll-free).

▽ *Many of the continental islands in the Whitsunday Passage are large, high and forested and look similar to the mainland coast. Hook Island, left, in the Whitsunday group, has an underwater observatory, seen extending from the peninsula. Hamilton Island is the most highly developed in the group but the resort facilities and jet airstrip take up only a small area of the island. Deer and kangaroos, freshwater and saltwater crocodiles, wombats, quokkas and dingoes, koalas and emus have been included in an 80-hectare fauna park.*

Hook Island

Hamilton Island

Hayman Island

A continental island of 360 hectares, Hayman has a calm, coral-encircled bay and white sandy beach. It can be reached by sea-plane from Proserpine (25 minutes) ; by boat from Hamilton Island (40 minutes) ; by launch from Shute Harbour (1½ hours). No day trips allowed.

Accommodation: 230 self-contained rooms and suites, with air conditioning, hairdryer, toiletries, bathrobes, colour TV, video, radio, personal safe, refrigerator, ISD telephone; spas in suites. Resort facilities include 24-hour room service, daily laundry and dry cleaning services, card room, 4 restaurants, fashion boutiques, club lounge, billiards room, library, hairdresser, pharmacy, swimming pool, saltwater filtered swimming lagoon, tennis court, bowling green, gymnasium, spa and health club, art gallery.
Dress: Smart casual by day; dressy at night.
Atmosphere: Elegant; sophisticated; exclusive.
Children's facilities: Child care centre.
Reef-related activities: Scuba-diving training school; complete dive shop; dive boat to Bait Reef. Coral viewing. Reef cruises with snorkelling and diving. Helicopter sightseeing. Sunset launch cruises. Snorkelling. Reef walking. Big game fishing trips.
Other activities: Swimming, tennis, bowls, sailing, water-skiing, para-sailing, paddle skis, windsurfing, catamarans, dinghies and outboards, fishing, birdwatching.
Tariff: Room only: $220–$395 per person twin share per night.
Contact: (079) 46 9100. (008) 07 5025 (toll-free).

Hook Island

The second largest of the Whitsundays group, Hook is a 2400-hectare continental island and a National Park where Aboriginal cave paintings can still be seen. It can be reached by catamaran from Shute Harbour (1 hour). It is also accessible for coach tour camping trips.

Accommodation: 12 camp cabins with 6 bed spaces; 50 tent sites. Facilities include a gift/souvenir shop, a coffee shop/store, licensed bar, electric barbecues.
Dress: Practical and casual.
Atmosphere: Casual.
Children's facilities: No special facilities; children welcome.
Reef-related activities: Coral and fish viewing from underwater observatory, in conditions of varying visibility due to the strong currents, and from semi-submersible. Snorkelling. Glass-bottom boat for coral viewing. Fish feeding.
Other activities: Paddle skis, bushwalking.
Tariff: Accommodation only: Bunk style cabins $15 per person per night; camping $7.50 per person per night.
Contact: (079) 46 9433.

Lindeman Island

This 800-hectare continental island has lush vegetation and seven sandy beaches with fringing reefs. It offers good birdwatching and 20 km of tree-lined walking tracks with some spectacular views. A National Park covers 500 hectares. Camping is not permitted. The island can be reached by boat from Hamilton Island (20 minutes) or from Shute Harbour (80 minutes) daily; by helicopter from Proserpine on most days (20 minutes); by air from Mackay daily (30 minutes); by air from Hamilton Island (10 minutes). No day trips allowed.

Accommodation: 104 self-contained units, with balcony, air conditioning, direct-dial telephone, mini-bar, tea and coffee making facilities, colour TV, video circuit. There are also 48 older-style rooms. Resort facilities include bars and restaurants, 9-hole golf course, swimming pool, day/night tennis courts.
Dress: Casual; smart casual at night.
Atmosphere: Unspoiled; families well catered for.
Children's facilities: Fully supervised daily program for 3–8-year-olds. Special dinner and evening program. Baby-sitting at normal rates. Camping out and bush craft program for 9–14-year-olds in supervised groups; 2-day camping trips ($15 per day plus meals extra).
Reef-related activities: Diving instruction; diving trips to Reef. Snorkelling. Glass-bottom boat. Reef cruises and flights. Cruises to other islands. Deep sea fishing.

▽ *A luxury resort has been built on the only flat land among Hayman Island's high ridges, and the lagoon and beach dredged to provide a constant depth of water. Hook Island, south of Hayman, can be seen in the background.*

▽ ▽ *Along with Brampton Island, Lindeman Island, in the foreground, is in the Cumberland group adjoining the Whitsundays, which spread to the north.*

Hayman Island

Lindeman Island

Long Island

South Molle Island

South Molle Island

◁ *The resort on South Molle Island takes up only a small area; the rest of the island is now a national park, slowly recovering from the days when the island was used for grazing. Because South Molle is close to the mainland, it was the first of the Whitsunday islands to be settled, and its sheltered beaches are a focus for many sporting activities.*

△ *A favourite spot for bushwalkers, Long Island is in the Molle Channel. The resort at Palm Bay is essentially a camping facility. Another resort at Happy Bay, the island's northern beach, has full hotel facilities.*

Other activities: Beach disco, water-skiing, tennis, golf, swimming, windsurfing, para-sailing, sailing, catamarans, paddle skis, jet skis, runabouts, mountain hikes (up Mt Oldfield), cricket, aerobics, volleyball, trampoline, bushwalking.
Tariff: All inclusive (except liquor, fuel-powered sporting equipment, charters): $90–$130 per person twin share per day. There is an optional room only tariff (meals a la carte): $41–$81.
Contact: (079) 46 9333. (008) 77 7322 (toll-free).

Long Island

A National Park with thick rainforest, Long Island is 103 hectares with pleasant beaches fringed with coconut palms and a dredged lagoon. There are two separately run and quite different resorts: at Palm Bay and at Happy Bay. The island can be reached by boat from Hamilton Island (30 minutes) or Shute Harbour (50 minutes).

Accommodation: Palm Bay offers 9 cabins with kitchen facilities; camping facilities; barbecues, shower block, shop/kiosk. At the resort at Happy Bay there are 145 self-contained units, with fans, tea and coffee making facilities, stereo radio. Resort facilities include coffee shop, bars, disco, gymnasium, boutique, swimming pool, tennis courts, fitness track and games lounge.
Dress: At Palm Bay, practical and casual; at Happy Bay, dressy casual at night.
Atmosphere: Palm Bay caters for families; relaxed and secluded. Happy Bay is friendly and outgoing – aimed specifically at 18-35s.

South Molle Island

Children's facilities: Children not catered for at Happy Bay.
Reef-related activities: Snorkelling at Palm Bay. Scuba diving and snorkelling lessons and reef cruises at Happy Bay.
Other activities: Swimming in all-tide lagoon, dinghy hire, fishing, oyster picking, bushwalking at Palm Bay. Swimming, tennis, archery, water-skiing, catamarans, windsurfing, mini yachts, para-sailing, rainforest hiking and aerobics at Happy Bay.
Tariff: Palm Bay: $70 per night per cabin (6-8 beds); hostel accommodation $15 per night; equipped tents $10-$14 per night.
Happy Bay: All inclusive (except liquor, fuel-powered sporting equipment, charters): $105 per person twin share per day.
Contact: Palm Bay (079) 46 9233.
Happy Bay (079) 46 9400.

South Molle Island

South Molle is a secluded, 405-hectare hilly continental island of bays, beaches and inlets offering protected anchorage. The hilltops in this National Park provide spectacular views over the Whitsunday Passage; though the vegetation in many areas is sparse – the result of over-grazing in earlier days – it is gradually recovering.The island can be reached by boat from Shute Harbour twice daily (25 minutes); by boat from Hamilton Island (55 minutes); by helicopter from Hamilton Island (15 minutes). Camping is not permitted.

Accommodation: 202 self-contained units ranging from beachfront to budget cabins, with air conditioning, tea and coffee making facilities, refrigerator, video, radio, direct dial telephone. Resort facilities include shops, gymnasium, bar, restaurant, half Olympic-size freshwater swimming pool, squash court, 2 tennis courts, 9-hole golf course, sauna, spa, laundry and hairdresser.
Dress: Casual.
Atmosphere: Non-stop professionally organised entertainment and activities; caters largely for young families.
Children's facilities: Playground. Nursery, child-minding centre. Cots and high chairs available. Activities and competitions organised daily. Baby-sitting at normal rates.
Reef-related activities: Scuba diving instruction available. Coral submarine. Reef cruises. Game fishing trips.
Other activities: Tennis, swimming, golf, squash, para-sailing, aqua bikes, volleyball, paddle skis, windsurfing, water-skiing, sailing.
Tariff: All inclusive (except liquor, fuel-powered sporting equipment, charters): $105–$150 per person twin share per day.
Contact: (079) 46 9433. (008) 07 5080 (toll-free).

The Tropical islands

There are eight islands with resorts in the Cairns section of the Great Barrier Reef Marine Park: Bedarra, Dunk, Fitzroy, Green, Hinchinbrook, Lizard, Magnetic and Orpheus. Only one – Green Island – is on the Reef itself. There is also a 'pontoon' island – the world's only floating hotel – moored in a lagoon on John Brewer Reef.

During winter and spring, temperatures reach 26°C–30°C by day and fall pleasantly at night. In summer, average maximum is about 32°C. Summer nights stay hot; there is persistent rain January to March and often intolerable humidity. Lowest temperature is about 17°C in July.

Townsville (1380 km N of Brisbane; daily flights and weekly MotorRail service from Brisbane) is Queensland's second largest city and is an access point for Bedarra, Dunk, Hinchinbrook, Magnetic and Orpheus Islands, and the resort hotel on John Brewer Reef. The city boasts the world's largest live coral reef aquarium, and offers day trips to the Reef, game fishing trips, mainland package tours including Reef visits, and daily flights to Dunk Island.

Lucinda (1520 km N of Brisbane, 27 km E of Ingham; daily flights to Townsville, then bus) is an access point for Orpheus Island. Most visitors to Lucinda come to launch boats for fishing or scenic cruising around Hinchinbrook or the Palm Islands, but the town has another claim to fame – a 6 km pier built out over the tidal mudflats.

Cardwell (1545 km N of Brisbane, 52 km N of Ingham; train from Brisbane most days) is an access point for Hinchinbrook Island. The town has glorious views of Hinchinbrook Passage and also offers day trips to the island. Cardwell is popular as a base for island holidays or pleasure cruising; as the sea in the area is often muddy, there are freshwater pools in the town.

Mission Beach (1626 km N of Brisbane, 25 km E of Tully; daily bus from Cairns) is one of the access points for Dunk Island. It also has holiday resorts, a reef aquarium and spectacular views of Dunk and Bedarra Islands. There are three beaches in the area, along 14 km of palm-fringed shoreline, one of the only surviving areas of lowland rainforest in the tropics. More than a dozen tropical islands are within easy reach by launch or water taxi; the Reef is 55 minutes away by fast catamaran.

Cairns (1757 km N of Brisbane; daily flights and weekly MotorRail services) is Queensland's most northerly city and an access point for Bedarra, Dunk, Fitzroy, Green, Hinchinbrook and Lizard Islands. With its international airport, Cairns is also the starting point for trips to the Far North and the beautiful Tableland district, and home of the game fishing fleet from September to December.

Cairns offers many opportunities for day trips: by boat to Green Island and/or Michaelmas Cay; catamaran cruises to Fitzroy Island and Outer Reef; 20-minute cruises to Low Isles on the Reef; cruises to Dunk Island and to the uninhabited Brook Islands; fishing launch trips and scuba-diving charters. There is also a day cruise to Townsville (first stop Dunk Island, then past Bedarra Island, through Hinchinbrook Channel and the Palm Islands to Magnetic Island and Townsville); the trip is reversed on alternate days. There are regular flights to Dunk Island; flights to Cooktown and Lizard Island; helicopter flights over the Reef. All day and overnight trips depart from Cairns marina. The natural harbour (Trinity Inlet) offers safe anchorage for small boats.

Cooktown (334 km N of Cairns; buses from Cairns three times a week) is an access point for Lizard Island and for trips to the Cape York Peninsula; combined package tours are available.

▽ *Gateway to several of the resort islands in the northern section of the Great Barrier Reef, Townsville, left, has a busy protected harbour for pleasure craft dominated by a new casino and hotel complex to cater for mainland tourists. The far-north tropical town of Cooktown, spreading alongside the mangrove flats of the Endeavour River, plays host to visitors heading for Cape York, and is the nearest town to the national park and resort on Lizard Island.*

Townsville

Cooktown

Bedarra (Richards) Island

Part of the Family Islands group, Bedarra is a privately owned 100-hectare continental island of mountains, rainforest and beaches. It can be reached by boat from Dunk Island (20 minutes); by charter boat from Cairns or Townsville; by air from Cairns (30 minutes) or Townsville (50 minutes) to Dunk Island, then boat. There are two related resorts set at opposite ends of the island and connected by a walking trail.

Accommodation: 32 self-contained villa-style units (16 at each resort), with air conditioning, ISD direct-dial telephone, ceiling fan, hair dryer, radio. Resort facilities include restaurants, 24-hour bars, full laundry service, tennis courts, freshwater swimming pools and spas.
Dress: Smart casual by day; more dressy at night.
Atmosphere: Secluded; exclusive.
Children's facilities: Children under the age of 15 not catered for.
Reef-related activities: Reef cruises and diving courses via Dunk Island (6.5 km away). Snorkelling (quite good; water can be murky). Game fishing charters.
Other activities: Tennis, swimming, catamarans, windsurfing, outboard dinghies, paddle skis, fishing.
Tariff: All inclusive (including liquor and all on-island activities): $300 per person per night.
Contact: Bookings through Australian Airlines.

Dunk Island

This 1200-hectare continental island of hilly rainforest and golden sands, with a functioning dairy farm, is part of the Family Islands. More than half the island – 730 hectares – is a National Park, with the highest peak Mount Koo-tal-oo at 271 metres. Dunk can be reached by air from Cairns (40 minutes) or Townsville (45 minutes); by water taxi from Mission Beach daily (15 minutes). Day trips are available.

Accommodation: 153 self-contained beachfront and garden units and cabanas, with refrigerator, tea and coffee making facilities. Resort facilities include golf course, 3 swimming pools and spa, 3 tennis courts, 2 squash courts, boutique, hairdressing salon, guest laundry, disco, restaurants, TV and video lounge, valet laundry service, public telephones.
Dress: Casual by day (tops required in restaurant and lounge); smart casual or dressy at night (slacks and open shirts for men; no thongs).

▷ *Officially called Richards Island, Bedarra, top, is one of many small, coral-fringed islands of the Family group. Dunk Island has a forest-clad ridge which separates the national park from the resort overlooking Brammo Bay in the western part of the island. Rainforest fringes a number of narrow beaches, some accessible only by boat.*

Bedarra (Richards) Island

Dunk Island

Fitzroy Island

◁ *Fitzroy Island is a continental island ringed by coral shingle beaches backed by a prolific growth of rainforest, which is also a dominant inland feature of Bedarra Island, below, where the walking trail between the two resorts offers a cool retreat.*

Bedarra (Richards) Island

Atmosphere: Popular with wide cross-section of holiday-makers.

Children's facilities: Children's club with daily activities for 3–13-year-olds. Playground. High chairs in restaurant. Free pony rides at farm. Early dinner service, with free child-minding for children 3 and over until 9 pm. Strollers, baby baths and nappy buckets available. Baby-sitting at normal rates.

Reef-related activities: Snorkelling. Scuba-diving and lessons; catamaran trip to Reef with scuba diving for certified divers only. Coral viewing by glass-bottom boat or submersible. Reef cruises to Beaver Cay (which offers good diving). Sailing cruises. Game fishing charters.

Other activities: Swimming, tennis, squash, golf, indoor cricket, archery, guided garden walks, catamarans, paddle skis, farm visits, rainforest walks, birdwatching, para-sailing, water-skiing, horse riding, clay target shooting, dinghies with outboards, aerobics, indoor bowls, table tennis, volleyball, water tobogganing, 4 swimming beaches, visits to artists colony, indoor games, jogging paths.

Tariff: All inclusive (except liquor, fuel-powered sporting equipment, charters, optional a la carte restaurant): $140-$187 per person twin share per day.

Contact: Bookings through Australian Airlines.

Fitzroy Island

This mountainous 324-hectare continental island offers lush tropical rainforest, volcanic outcrops, streams and waterfalls, coral shingle beaches and calm water. The island can be reached by catamaran from Cairns (45 minutes). Day trips are available.

Accommodation: Eight self-contained villa units; 32 hostel-style bunkhouse units with communal facilities; public camping grounds. Resort facilities include bars, swimming pool, spa.

Atmosphere: Casual.

Children's facilities: Children welcome; no special facilities.

Reef-related activities: Semi-submersible and catamaran cruises to Moore Reef. Diving. Snorkelling. Coral viewing from glass-bottom, semi-submersible.

Other activities: Bushwalking, canoes, paddle skis, swimming at all-tide coarse coral sand beach and sheltered bay, boating, fishing, water bikes, lighthouse walk, visits to clam farm.

Tariff: Villa-units (dinner, bed & breakfast): from $99 per person per day; bunkhouses (four sharing): $23 per person per day; 10 camping sites $10.00 per day.

Contact: Resort (070) 51 9588; Camping ground (070) 51 0455.

▷ *At the end of the Green Island jetty is an underwater observatory. As the island is a coral cay on the reef itself, the observatory offers many glimpses of the wonders of coral marine life.*

▽ *Granite boulders stud the beaches of Lizard Island, a national park and the northernmost resort in the Cairns section of the Great Barrier Reef Marine Park.*

Lizard Island

Green Island

Green Island

A 13-hectare coral cay, Green Island was the first on the Barrier Reef to have a resort. Formed by the accumulation of rubble and sediments from its platform reef, the island – while only 1 metre above sea level – has rainforest, pandanus and casuarinas, soft sandy beaches and clear water. It is a National Park and all plants and wildlife are protected; fishing and spearfishing are forbidden. Green can be reached by catamaran from Cairns daily (40 minutes); by launch from Cairns daily (90 minutes). Day trips are available.

Accommodation: 28 self-contained units in cabin and lodge style, with patio, tea and coffee making facilities, colour TV, mini-bar; cabins also have refrigerator and private patio.
Dress: Casual.
Atmosphere: Crowded with day trippers; secluded and relaxed after 4 pm.
Children's facilities: Special children's dinner. Movies from 7 pm–8.30 pm (parents' dinner time).
Reef-related activities: Guided reef walks. Snorkelling trips and lessons. Coral viewing by glass-bottom boat. Canoe trips around island. Underwater observatory trips. Scuba diving courses and trips to other reefs (local diving is no longer good as the reef has been affected by the crown-of-thorns starfish).

Outer Reef cruises to Michaelmas Cay. Marineland museum-aquarium. Reef movies and videos; filmed dive.
Other activities: Bush walks, birdwatching, basketball, archery, volleyball.
Tariff: Dinner, bed and breakfast: $99–$110 per person twin share per day.
Contact: (070) 51 4644.

Hinchinbrook Island

Largest of the continental islands off the Queensland coast, Hinchinbrook, at 39 350 hectares, is also the world's largest island National Park. It is a wilderness area of volcanic peaks, dense tropical rainforest, eucalypt forest and mangroves, with 11 sandy beaches. Birds, wallabies and goannas abound. There is a resort at Cape Richards (Orchid Bay) at the tip of the north-eastern arm. The island can be reached by seaplane from Townsville (30 minutes); by seaplane from Cairns (45 minutes); by launch from Cardwell (30 minutes). Day trips are available.

Accommodation: 12 free-standing cabins (bedroom, bathroom, living room, sundeck) with tea and coffee making facilities. Resort facilities include a licensed bar, lending library of books and magazines, laundry facilities and a shop.

Hinchinbrook Island

△ *Mangrove swamps, such as those on Hinchinbrook Island, provide nutrients for the reef's food chain.*

▷ *Mecca for big-game fishing charters, Lizard Island has splendid coral reefs, a giant clam garden, and a research station operated by the Australian Museum.*

Dress: Casual.
Atmosphere: Casual and relaxed; secluded.
Children's facilities: Early meals can be arranged. Child-minding.
Reef-related activities: Snorkelling. Scuba diving. Cruises to uninhabited islands and to reef gardens of the Brook Islands daily, weather and tide permitting.
Other activities: Bush walks, fishing, sailing, windsurfing, oyster picking, birdwatching, freshwater pool swimming, dinghies, excursions to other parts of island, surf skiing, canoes.
Tariff: All inclusive (except liquor, charters): $120-$150 per person twin share per day.
Contact: (070) 66 8585. (008) 77 7021 (toll-free).

John Brewer Reef

An off-shore floating hotel is moored in a 1350-hectare lagoon, creating a 'pontoon' island. The shallow central lagoon — with an average water depth of 8 metres — is almost totally encircled by coral outcrops. There is an abundance of fish life. The reef is 72 km northeast of Townsville and can be reached by highspeed catamaran twice daily (90 minutes) or by helicopter charter (20 minutes) from Townsville. Day visitors are welcome (with a small charge for casual mooring).

Accommodation: 200 self-contained rooms and suites, with air conditioning, colour television, direct-dial telephone, in-house video movies, mini-bar, refrigerator. Resort facilities include 24-hour room service, two restaurants, three bars, nightclub/disco, gift shop, pharmacy, swimming pool, tennis court, sauna, gymnasium.
Dress: Smart casual by day; more dressy at night.
Atmosphere: Elegant; exclusive.
Children's facilities: Videos, gym classes, afternoon disco. Cots available. Babysitting at normal rates.
Reef-related activities: Coral viewing in a semi-submersible submarine. Underwater observatory. Snorkelling and scuba diving lessons; excursions and night dives. Fish feeding. Glass-bottom paddle boards. Game fishing charters. Yacht cruises, catamaran cruises. Helicopter sightseeing flights. Visits to other islands.
Other activities: Swimming, tennis, sailing, windsurfing, catamarans, paddle-wheel boats.
Tariff: $175 – $320 per person twin share per day.
Contact: (077) 70 9111. (008) 02 3181 (toll-free).

Lizard Island

The northernmost island resort in Australia, this 1012-hectare National Park island features rainforest, a palm grove, pandanus forest, a granite peak, 24 beaches surrounded by fringing reef – and harmless Monitor Lizards. There is a marine research facility on the Blue Lagoon. The island can be reached by air from Cairns daily (1 hour); by air from Cooktown (20 minutes). Day trips are available.

Lizard Island

Accommodation: 30 self-contained cabins, with air conditioning, balcony, mini-bar, ironing facilities; two have separate living areas. Resort facilities include a shop, lounge and bar, dining room, tennis court, swimming pool.

Dress: Smart casual; dressy casual at night.

Atmosphere: Relaxed; intimate; exclusive; popular with big-game fishing groups.

Children's facilities: Children under 6 not catered for.

Reef-related activities: Good reef walking. Excellent dive course; dive boat; island is adjacent to the best single dive on the Reef (Cormorant Pass on No 10 Ribbon Reef). Good snorkelling. Outer Reef cruises. Glass-bottom boat. Big game fishing trips from August to December.

Other activities: Water-skiing, catamarans, windsurfing, dinghies, mountain hikes, beach fishing, tennis, swimming, bushwalking, archery, paddle skis, canoes, birdwatching, lizard watching.

Tariff: Inclusive (except liquor, laundry service and charters): $266-$316 per person twin share per day.

Contact: Bookings through Australian Airlines.

Magnetic Island

Three-quarters of this mountainous continental island of 5184 hectares is a National Park, with palm groves, secluded bays, tropical beaches and rocky headlands. It can be reached by passenger and vehicular ferry from Townsville (40 minutes). Day trips are available.

Accommodation: Resorts and settlements all around the island, with hotels, motels, guest houses, self-contained flats, cabins and camping grounds. Restaurants, shops, vehicle hire, golf and bowls clubs, taxi service, bus service, banks, TV and video hire and TAB.

Dress: Casual.

Atmosphere: Resort suburb of Townsville; low-key island for family holidays.

Children's facilities: According to choice of accommodation.

Reef-related activities: Snorkelling. Daily reef cruises (for fishing, snorkelling and coral viewing). Big-game fishing trips.

Other activities: Bushwalking, horse riding, jet skiing, sailing, para-sailing, 4-wheel drive mini tours, catamarans, windsurfing, water-skiing, golf, bicycling, lawn bowls, paddle boats, canoes, tennis, water taxi, mountain hikes.

Tariff: According to style of accommodation.

Contact: Queensland Government Travel Centre.

Orpheus Island

Just over half of this 2200-hectare continental island is a National Park, and there is a research station for giant clam farming on the island, as well as a colony of wild goats. There are seven secluded beaches with fringing coral, and low rainforest behind. Orpheus

Orpheus Island

Michaelmas Cay

◁▽ *Uninhabited coral cays – such as Michaelmas Cay provide safe nesting grounds for thousands of seabirds and are popular day-trip destinations from many resorts.*

◁ *Orpheus, in the Palm Islands, has secluded granite-strewn beaches, a research station, and a private resort. Named after a naval warship which was later wrecked in New Zealand, the island is also home to a colony of wild goats, below, survivors of other shipwrecks.*

Orpheus Island

can be reached by chartered helicopter from Townsville (20 minutes); by seaplane from Townsville (20 minutes); by boat from Lucinda (2 hours). No day trips are allowed.

Accommodation: 25 self-contained studio units, with air conditioning, refrigerator, bar, tea and coffee making facilities, sound system and radio; bungalow units have bath tub and private courtyard garden. Resort facilities include shop/boutique, laundry service, freshwater swimming pool and spa, tennis court.
Dress: Smart casual; more dressy at night.
Atmosphere: Relaxed; secluded; exclusive.
Children's facilities: Children 12 and under not catered for.
Reef-related activities: Snorkelling. Full-day island cruises (weather permitting). Coral viewing. Scuba diving; resort dive course. Cruising charters. Reef cruises. Glass-bottom boat. Offshore fishing; big game fishing trips.
Other activities: Fishing, swimming (in pool), tennis, catamaran sailing, windsurfing, paddle boards, outboard runabouts, island walks, after-dinner cruises, Laser sailboat, water-skiing.
Tariff: All inclusive (except liquor, fuel-powered sporting equipment, charters): $230–$250 per person twin share per day (minimum stay 3 nights).
Contact: (077) 77 7377.

Where to book your Barrier Reef holiday

For package tours, accommodation and all travel requirements – air, coach and train – bookings for all the resorts and mainland towns and cities mentioned in this book can be made through your local travel agent, any branch of Australian Airlines (where specified) or through the Queensland Tourist Corporation and associated travel centres at the following addresses.

All information was correct at the time of going to press.

Queensland Government Travel Centres

Brisbane Queensland
196 Adelaide Street, Brisbane 4000.
Phone (07) 833 5400. Telex 40235
Facsimile (07) 221 5320

Newcastle New South Wales
516 Hunter Street, Newcastle 2300.
Phone (049) 26 2800. Telex 28177

Sydney New South Wales
75 Castlereagh Street, Sydney 2000.
Phone (02) 232 1788. Telex 120404
Facsimile (02) 231 5153

Canberra ACT
25 Garema Place, Canberra City 2601.
Phone (062) 48 8411

Melbourne Victoria
257 Collins Street, Melbourne 3000.
Phone (03) 654 3866. Telex 30200
Facsimile (03) 650 1847

Adelaide South Australia
10 Grenfell Street, Adelaide 5000.
Phone (08) 212 2399

Perth Western Australia
55 St George's Terrace, Perth 6000.
Phone (09) 325 1600

Queensland Holiday Shop

Parramatta New South Wales
309 Church Street, Parramatta 2150.
Phone (02) 891 1966

State & Corporate Travel Centre

Brisbane Queensland
Cnr Adelaide and Edward Streets, Brisbane 4000.
Phone (07) 229 5222. Telex 40235
Facsimile (07) 221 5320

Queensland Travel & Tourist Corporation

Brisbane Queensland
123 Eagle Street, Brisbane 4000.
Phone (07) 833 5400. Telex 42821
Facsimile (07) 833 5436

Overseas Representatives

Auckland New Zealand
9th floor, Quay Tower
29 Customs Street West, Auckland
Phone (09) 39 6421. Telex 746 0945
Facsimile (09) 77 9439

London United Kingdom
Queensland House
392/3 Strand, London
Phone (01) 836 1333. Telex 51 268905
Facsimile (01) 240 7667

Los Angeles USA
611 North Larchmont Boulevard, Los Angeles.
Phone (213) 465 8418. Telex 25 188392
Facsimile (213) 465 5815

Vancouver Canada
Phone (604) 737 7721
Facsimile (604) 737 7644

New York USA
636 Fifth Avenue, New York
Phone (212) 969 9560
Facsimile (212) 969 9581

Singapore
101 Thomson Road, Goldhill Square, Singapore
Phone (65) 253 2811. Telex 87 28181
Facsimile (65) 253 8653

Munich Germany
Phone (089) 260 9693. Telex 41 521 8855
Facsimile (089) 260 3530

Tokyo Japan
8th floor, Sankaido Building,
9-13 Akasaka 1-Chome, Minato-Ku, Tokyo
Phone (03) 582 4431. Telex 720 2427509
Facsimile (03) 589 5352

Camping permits

Permits are required for camping in non-resort areas on National Park islands of the Great Barrier Reef. For further information contact the National Parks and Wildlife Service at the relevant administration centre:

Brisbane: MLC Centre, 239 George Street, Brisbane, 4000.
Telephone: (07) 227 4111.
Cairns: 41 Esplanade, Cairns, 4870.
Telephone: (070) 51 9811.
Mackay: PO Box 623, Mackay, 4740.
Telephone: (079) 57 6292.
Rockhampton: 194 Quay Street, Rockhampton, 4700.
Telephone: (079) 27 6070.
Townsville: PO Box 5391, Mail Centre, Townsville, 4810.
Telephone: (077) 74 1332.

Islands & resorts at a glance

Island	Access	Size	Distance from reef	No. of guests	Camping	Day trips	Aerobics	Aqua-bikes	Archery	Badminton	Ball games	Billiards	Birdwatching	Boating
Bedarra	Cairns, Dunk Island, Townsville	100 ha.	32 km	64										✓
Brampton	Mackay	78 ha.	50 km	300		✓	✓	✓	✓		✓	✓	✓	
Daydream	Hamilton Island, Shute Harbour	11 ha.	56 km	200		✓				✓	✓	✓		✓
Dunk	Cairns, Mission Beach, Townsville	1200 ha.	35 km	320	✓ (not at resort)	✓	✓		✓		✓		✓	✓
Fitzroy	Cairns	324 ha.	13 km	30 (+ campers)	✓	✓			✓					✓
Great Keppel	Rockhampton, Rosslyn Bay	1454 ha.	40 km	400	✓ (not at resort)	✓	✓	✓	✓	✓	✓			✓
Green	Cairns	13 ha.	On Reef	80		✓			✓		✓		✓	
Hamilton	Direct flights to island	607 ha.	75 km	1400		✓	✓					✓		✓
Hayman	Hamilton Island, Proserpine, Shute Harbour	360 ha.	29 km	480								✓	✓	✓
Heron	Gladstone	17 ha.	On Reef	250		✓						✓	✓	
Hinchinbrook	Cairns, Cardwell, Townsville	39 350 ha.	8 km	30	✓ (not at resort)	✓							✓	✓
Hook	Shute Harbour	2400 ha.	29 km	72	✓	✓								
John Brewer Reef	Townsville	7 km × 3 km	On Reef	400 (floating hotel)		✓								
Lady Elliot	Bundaberg	42 ha.	On Reef	136						✓				
Lady Musgrave	Bundaberg	14 ha.	On Reef	–	✓	✓							✓	
Lindeman	Hamilton Island, Mackay, Proserpine, Shute Harbour	800 ha.	80 km	400				✓			✓		✓	✓
Lizard	Cairns, Cooktown	1012 ha.	16 km	64	✓ (not at resort)	✓			✓				✓	✓
Long	Hamilton Island, Shute Harbour	103 ha.	66 km	500 (+ campers)	✓	✓		✓	✓	✓				✓
Magnetic	Townsville	52 sq. km.	48 km	1200 (approx)		✓	✓						✓	✓
Orpheus	Lucinda, Townsville	2200 ha.	15 km	50										✓
South Molle	Hamilton Island, Proserpine, Shute Harbour	405 ha.	56 km	630					✓		✓			

Boom-netting	Bushwalking	Clay-target shooting	Coral viewing	Diving	Diving trips	Fishing	Fishing trips	Golf	Gymnasium	Horse riding	Jogging	Lawn bowls	Paddle skis	Para-sailing	Reef walking	Sailing	Snorkelling	Squash	Swimming	Table tennis	Tennis	Water games	Water-skiing	Windsurfing		Anchorage	Boat charters	Dive shop	Evening entertainment	Glass-bottom boat	Island cruises	Private aircraft	Reef cruises	Reef flights	Semi-submersible	Underwater observatory
	✓					✓	✓						✓			✓	✓		✓		✓			✓									✓			
	✓		✓		✓	✓	✓	✓	✓		✓		✓		✓	✓	✓		✓	✓	✓		✓	✓					✓	✓	✓		✓	✓		
✓	✓		✓	✓	✓	✓	✓						✓	✓		✓	✓		✓	✓	✓		✓	✓		✓	✓	✓	✓	✓	✓		✓	✓	✓	✓
	✓	✓	✓	✓	✓		✓	✓		✓	✓		✓	✓		✓	✓		✓	✓	✓	✓	✓			✓	✓		✓	✓	✓				✓	
	✓		✓		✓	✓							✓			✓			✓							✓	✓		✓				✓		✓	
✓	✓		✓	✓	✓	✓		✓			✓		✓	✓		✓	✓	✓	✓	✓	✓	✓	✓			✓	✓	✓	✓	✓	✓		✓			
	✓		✓		✓	✓									✓		✓		✓							✓		✓		✓			✓			✓
	✓		✓						✓				✓	✓		✓	✓	✓	✓	✓	✓	✓	✓	✓		✓	✓			✓	✓		✓	✓	✓	✓
	✓	✓	✓	✓	✓		✓		✓			✓	✓	✓	✓	✓		✓		✓		✓	✓			✓	✓	✓	✓			✓	✓	✓	✓	✓
	✓		✓	✓	✓		✓								✓		✓		✓	✓	✓					✓	✓	✓				✓	✓		✓	✓
	✓		✓			✓										✓	✓		✓				✓			✓	✓			✓			✓			
	✓		✓										✓			✓	✓		✓							✓			✓						✓	✓
	✓		✓	✓	✓		✓			✓			✓		✓	✓	✓		✓	✓			✓			✓		✓	✓			✓	✓	✓	✓	✓
	✓		✓	✓	✓		✓				✓				✓		✓		✓							✓			✓							
	✓		✓	✓										✓			✓		✓							✓			✓				✓			
	✓		✓		✓		✓	✓					✓	✓		✓	✓		✓		✓		✓	✓		✓	✓	✓	✓		✓		✓	✓		
	✓		✓	✓	✓	✓	✓								✓	✓	✓		✓		✓		✓	✓		✓	✓	✓		✓			✓			
	✓			✓		✓			✓		✓				✓		✓		✓		✓		✓	✓		✓		✓					✓			
	✓				✓	✓	✓		✓		✓					✓	✓		✓		✓		✓	✓		✓	✓	✓					✓			
	✓		✓	✓		✓	✓	✓					✓	✓		✓	✓	✓	✓	✓	✓		✓	✓		✓	✓	✓					✓		✓	

Index

Page numbers in italic indicate illustrations

Printed in 1988 by Dai Nippon Printing Co Ltd,
Hong Kong, for Reader's Digest Services
Pty Ltd (Inc in NSW), 26-32 Waterloo Street,
Surry Hills, NSW 2010, Australia.